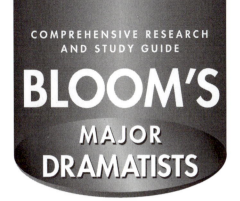

COMPREHENSIVE RESEARCH
AND STUDY GUIDE

BLOOM'S
MAJOR
DRAMATISTS

Thornton Wilder

EDITED AND WITH AN
INTRODUCTION BY HAROLD BLOOM

CURRENTLY AVAILABLE

BLOOM'S MAJOR DRAMATISTS

Aeschylus
Aristophanes
Bertolt Brecht
Anton Chekhov
Euripides
Henrik Ibsen
Eugène Ionesco
Ben Jonson
Christopher Marlowe
Arthur Miller
Molière
Eugene O'Neill
Luigi Pirandello
Shakespeare's Comedies
Shakespeare's Histories
Shakespeare's Romances
Shakespeare's Tragedies
George Bernard Shaw
Sam Shepard
Neil Simon
Tom Stoppard
Sophocles
Oscar Wilde
Thornton Wilder
Tennessee Williams
August Wilson

COMPREHENSIVE RESEARCH
AND STUDY GUIDE

BLOOM'S
MAJOR
DRAMATISTS

Thornton Wilder

EDITED AND WITH AN INTRODUCTION
BY HAROLD BLOOM

CHELSEA HOUSE
PUBLISHERS
A Haights Cross Communications Company

Philadelphia

A Haights Cross Communications ⬥ Company

Introduction © 2003 by Harold Bloom.

Printed and bound in the United States of America.

First Printing
1 3 5 7 9 8 6 4 2

Library of Congress Cataloging-in-Publication Data
Thornton Wilder / Harold Bloom, editor; Portia Williams Weiskel, contributing editor
    p. cm. — (Bloom's major dramatists)
Includes bibliographical references and index.
  ISBN 0-7910-7033-6
  1. Wilder, Thorton, 1897–1975—Criticism and interpretation. I.
Bloom, Harold. II. Weiskel, Portia Williams. III. Series.
  PS3545.I345 Z948
  818'.5209—dc21   2002008255

Chelsea House Publishers
1974 Sproul Road, Suite 400
Broomall, PA 19008-0914

http://www.chelseahouse.com

Contributing Editor: Portia Williams Weiskel

Cover designed by Terry Mallon

Layout by EJB Publishing Services

CONTENTS

USER'S GUIDE

This volume is designed to present biographical, critical, and bibliographical information on the author and the author's best-known or most important plays. Following Harold Bloom's editor's note and introduction is a concise biography of the author that discusses major life events and important literary accomplishments. A critical analysis of each play follows, tracing significant themes, patterns, and motifs in the work. An annotated list of characters supplies brief information on the main characters in each play.

A selection of critical extracts, derived from previously published material, follows each thematic analysis. In most cases, these extracts represent the best analysis available from a number of leading critics. Because these extracts are derived from previously published material, they will include the original notations and references when available. Each extract is cited, and readers are encouraged to use the original publications as they continue their research. A bibliography of the author's writings, a list of additional books and articles on the author and their work, and an index of themes and ideas conclude the volume.

As with any study guide, this volume is designed as a supplement to the works being discussed, and is in no way intended as a replacement for those works. The reader is advised to read the text prior to using this study guide, and to keep it accessible for quick reference.

ABOUT THE EDITOR

Harold Bloom is Sterling Professor of the Humanities at Yale University and Henry W. and Albert A. Berg Professor of English at the New York University Graduate School. He is the author of over 20 books, and the editor of more than 30 anthologies of literary criticism.

Professor Bloom's works include *Shelly's Mythmaking* (1959), *The Visionary Company* (1961), *Blake's Apocalypse* (1963), *Yeats* (1970), *A Map of Misreading* (1975), *Kabbalah and Criticism* (1975), *Agon: Toward a Theory of Revisionism* (1982), *The American Religion* (1992), *The Western Canon* (1994), and *Omens of Millennium: The Gnosis of Angels, Dreams, and Resurrection* (1996). *The Anxiety of Influence* (1973) sets forth Professor Bloom's provocative theory of the literary relationships between the great writers and their predecessors. His most recent books include *Shakespeare: The Invention of the Human*, a 1998 National Book Award finalist, *How to Read and Why* (2000), and *Stories and Poems for Extremely Intelligent Children of All Ages* (2001).

Professor Bloom earned his Ph.D. from Yale University in 1955 and has served on the Yale faculty since then. He is a 1985 MacArthur Foundation Award recipient and served as the Charles Eliot Norton Professor of Poetry at Harvard University in 1987–88. In 1999 he was awarded the prestigious American Academy of Arts and Letters Gold Medal for Criticism. Professor Bloom is the editor of several other Chelsea House series in literary criticism, including BLOOM'S MAJOR SHORT STORY WRITERS, BLOOM'S MAJOR NOVELISTS, BLOOM'S MAJOR DRAMATISTS, BLOOM'S MODERN CRITICAL INTERPRETATIONS, BLOOM'S MODERN CRITICAL VIEWS, and BLOOM'S BIOCRITIQUES.

EDITOR'S NOTE

My Introduction centers upon *The Skin of Our Teeth*, noting its adroit transformations of James Joyce's influence upon Thornton Wilder.

General views of Wilder's dramas include Edmund Wilson's defense of Wilder against Michael Gold's Marxist critique, and Robert W. Corrigan's stress on the playwright's avoidance of psychology.

Our Town's effective use of the dead as characters is extolled by Mary McCarthy, while David Castronovo shrewdly indicates how difficult it is to appreciate *Our Town* in the age of the Counter-Culture.

The theatricality of *The Skin of our Teeth* is emphasized by John Gassner, who is seconded by Donald Haberman. The critics in the main admire the artifice of both plays, while feeling an anxiety lest Wilder's efforts at last will turn out to be period pieces.

Harold Bloom

Rereading *Our Town* and *The Matchmaker* in 2002 provides a very mixed literary experience. One sees the past glories, but does not feel them. It is rather like—for me anyway—reseeing Fellini movies I had enjoyed immensely several decades ago. Time's revenges are inexorable, and all debates about canonical survival are resolved pragmatically by the grim process in which popular works become Period Pieces.

Aside from a few of his shorter plays, Wilder's only prospect for survival is *The Skin of Our Teeth*, again in my wavering judgment. I remember participating in occasional seminars on *Finnegans Wake* led by Wilder when I was a graduate student at Yale in the early Fifties. Genial and well-informed, Wilder particularly moved one by his clear love for Joyce's great, always-to-be-neglected Book of the Night. Rereading *The Skin of Our Teeth*, the charm of those seminars returns to me. Wilder emphasized Joyce's skill in rendering different eras of time simultaneously, which is his principal debt in the Antrobus family saga to Joyce.

It is not that the play can hold up when read too closely against the impacted mosaic of *Finnegans Wake*, but then what could? The Earwickers are obviously larger and more multivalent than the Antrobuses: they are also more Shakespearean, because of Joyce's deliberate *agon* with "the Englishman." Great "Shapesphere" puns his way through the *Wake*, where the generational struggles and family romances overtly remake *Hamlet*. One might wish that Wilder had taken even more from *Finnegans Wake*: an overtone of *Hamlet* might help to relieve the banality of the Antrobus children or the eternally unfailing goodness of Mrs. Antrobus, who would be enlivened by a touch of that sexual magnet, Queen Gertrude.

Doubtless *The Skin of Our Teeth* still stages better than it reads, but I fear that its simplifications are not intensifications but reductions. Theatrically, we are now in the Age of Sam Shepard and Tony Kushner. Their intensifications yet may prove to lack permanence: our theater is still Artaud's, with his angry motto: "No more masterpieces."

Thornton Wilder

Thornton Wilder liked to recall a scene from his youth in which a teacher quieted the classroom by instructing the students to be still "just long enough to hear the world fall through space." According to Linda Simon, one of his biographers, Wilder reported that the students held their breath, hearing only the silence and a far-off train whistle. "Perhaps," wrote Simon in 1979, "Thornton Wilder listened longer." This experience of heightened noticing, of framing random and ordinary moments of life, is an effect Wilder later coveted and perfected for his audiences.

As a child, Wilder had many chances to stop, look, and wonder. He was born (April 17, 1897, in Madison, Wisconsin) into an educated, devout, and public-spirited family. Madison was not a small town, but the family had a nearby cottage on a lake which is recalled reverently in family letters. Memories of suppers on the porch with good food and conversation, the sound of wind in trees, and quiet moments under the stars at night bespeak a nourishing childhood that anticipates the benign family life of *Our Town*, Wilder's best-known play.

The frequent moves of the Wilder family provided wide boundaries and contrasts for Thornton's youthful imagination. At the age of nine, he lived in China for six months while his father performed diplomatic services and became involved in supporting the Central China Famine Relief Committee. Three years later Wilder returned to China with his siblings and unhappily attended a mission school in Chefoo. China's vastness and antiquity left an enduring impression, and Wilder's time there provided a first and memorable encounter with the human misery of famine. In Berkeley, California, where the family moved next, Wilder was a good student, studied Greek drama, and daydreamed about titles for plays he intended to write. In high school he successfully performed his own skits.

Family life was secure but not always easy for Wilder. His brother, Amos, took an approved of path that led to a professorship at Harvard, but paternal attentiveness was sometimes oppressive for

Thornton whose eclectic and literary interests were not regarded as sufficiently impressive. He was sent to Oberlin College because of its academic reputation and unworldly atmosphere, but later transferred to Yale where he won an award for his play *The Trumpet Shall Sound*. He graduated in 1920 and was remembered for his exceptional wit. His family, meanwhile, had also moved to New Haven. Entering adulthood, Wilder had family, education, and formative memories, but no single place to call home. His early plays showed influences of both urbanity and homespun simplicity.

After Yale, Wilder studied archeology in Rome. Letters conveyed the awe he experienced unearthing the past with his own hands. Discovering roads two thousand years old with separate identifiable layers deepened his awareness, begun in China, of the vastness of time and space. He imagined millions of people walking the roads centuries apart from each other—laughing, wondering, planning, and grieving—each leaving, literally, a mark. He likened the experience to that of being at both ends of a telescope, with the sense of his own significance permanently altered. Years later (November 6, 1961), in an interview with Arthur Gelb of the *Times,* Wilder said, "I am not interested in the ephemeral—such subjects as the adulteries of dentists. I am interested in those things that repeat and repeat and repeat in the lives of millions." What persists through the centuries is what preoccupied Wilder, and his literary accomplishments reflect this absorbing interest.

Wilder returned to the U.S. where his father had found him a job teaching French at Lawrenceville School in New Jersey. Despite his resistance to his father's efforts to organize his life, Wilder discovered he enjoyed teaching and permanently kept "educator" as the formal description of his life. During these years, he attended the MacDowell Colony of Artists in Peterborough, NH, met writers and actors, and published *The Cabala* (1922). National fame came with the publication of *The Bridge of San Luis Rey* (1927), which won the 1928 Pulitzer Prize. Wilder never married but stayed close to his family, especially after his father's death in 1936. His wide circle of friends included luminaries and ordinary people alike. Alfred Hitchcock solicited his ideas for screenplays and actress Ruth Gordon was a companion. Gertrude Stein—his closest and most influential friend—encouraged the formulation of his theory of drama based on his view of the theatre being the most effective way to share with another what it is like to be a human being. Wilder served in Intelligence during WWII, and, in 1950-51, delivered the prestigious and popular Norton lectures at Harvard on "American Characteristics in Literature."

Wilder sustained two public attacks in his career. A letter to *The New Republic* (October 22, 1930) from Michael Gold, a Marxist critic, accused Wilder of ignoring social injustices. Edmund Wilson and Sinclair Lewis, among others, defended him; Malcolm Cowley, himself a social critic, praised him for occupying the poet's position from which to articulate compassion for the plight of humanity, but Wilder was unproductive until *Our Town* was published (1938). He was later charged (and exonerated) with plagiarizing Joyce's *Finnegan's Wake* in *Skin of Our Teeth* (1942). He wrote seven novels, five full-length and many one-act plays, film scripts, and critical essays; won three Pulitzer prizes, several honorary degrees, and a Presidential Medal of Freedom (1963); was invited to read at the White House by President Kennedy; and frequently acted in his own plays. He is linked with the American playwrights Williams, O'Neill, and Miller, but his critical stature is uncertain. Edmund Wilson noted that his double success as a popular and critical writer put him in a cultural no-man's land and Malcolm Cowley suggested his competence in several genres made him hard to place. Wilder aged with difficulty, losing sight and hearing and suffering back pain, but his imagination stayed bright and high-spirited until he died in his sleep at home in New Haven in 1975. He hoped his ideas and innovations would influence the next generation of writers, but he was modest about his accomplishments. He wanted to be remembered as one who kept faith in people and shared a belief in something eternal that unites all life. In the January, 1958, *Atlantic Monthly*, Archibald MacCleish praised Wilder as a patriot who strengthened America using the "weapons of the spirit."

CRITICAL VIEWS ON
Thornton Wilder's Work

EDMUND WILSON ON THE WILDER-GOLD CONTROVERSY

[Edmund Wilson was the most prominent American man of letters of his time. He was a literary critic, lecturer, writer, and general arbiter of taste and perspective in American culture. His best-known works are *Axel's Castle* (1931), his first book of literary criticism, and *Shores of Light* (1952). The Wilder-Gold controversy began with a letter to *The New Republic* attacking Wilder for ignoring social issues. The letter set in motion a major controversy and generated so many letters that the magazine was eventually forced arbitrarily to end the exchange. Wilson was one of the editors at the time.]

PERHAPS NO OTHER literary article published in the *New Republic* has ever aroused so much controversy as Michael Gold's on Thornton Wilder. (. . .)

The Marxist critic of the type of Michael Gold must assume that the character of the literature produced during any period is determined by the economic position of the class for whom it is written. That economic and social factors do play a much larger part in molding people's ideals, and consequently in coloring their literature, than most people are willing to admit, we are perfectly ready to agree. Yet there are groups which cut through the social classes, and these tend to have an independent existence. The writers make a group of their own; the painters make a group of their own; the scientists make a group. And each of these groups has its own tradition, its own craft and body of doctrine which has been brought down to the present by practitioners that have come from a variety of classes through a variety of different societies. In dealing with a work of literature, we must consider it not only from the point of view of its significance in the social system, but also from the point of view of its craft. A Communist critic who, in reviewing a book, ignores the author's status as a craftsman is really, for purposes of propaganda, denying the dignity of human work.

A typical example of this is to be found in Upton Sinclair's *Mammonart:* in this book, he appraises the literature of the world with the social-economic touchstone, but then goes on to glorify without reserve the physicists in the California laboratories. Yet if the people exploring the atom should be regarded as disinterested intellectuals, why may not the poets be? And if the works of the poets are influenced by feudal patrons and bourgeois audiences, why may not the discoveries of the physicists be conditioned—as they probably are—by the outlook of the capitalist society which has supplied them with the money for their laboratories? Has not the artist as good a chance as the scientist of living up to a personal ideal! Mr. Sinclair and Mr. Gold ought to think about this. The author of *Jews Without Money*, especially, ought to recognize and confess how much he has in common with the author of *The Bridge of San Luis Rey*— sensitiveness to human contacts, a love of picturesque detail, a gift for molding firm prose into short comprehensive units, and even a touch of sentimentality. (. . .)

. . . Thornton Wilder owes a good deal to Proust—in fact, without being aware of it and though he is a writer of real originality, he has in a sense been a popularizer of Proust. (. . .)

. . . The malaise, the frustration, the misery, with which he and Proust both deal are the illnesses of the cultivated people in a capitalistic society, which neither the luxuries of the Ritz nor the up-to-date fragments of the past [...] to be found in the fascinating antique shops and galleries can do more than deaden a little. The pathos in Proust, after all, is merely the more presentable side of the impotence, the creeping corruption, the lack of the will to live. And so in Wilder the pathos and the beauty derived from exotic lands of the imagination may be, as Michael Gold suggests, a sedative for sick Americans. The sedative and the demand for it are both products of the same situation: a people disposed to idealism, but deprived of their original ideals and now making themselves neurotic in the attempt to introduce idealism into the occupations— organizing, financing, manufacturing, advertising, salesmanship— of a precarious economic system the condition for whose success is that they must cut the throats of their neighbors and swindle one another. (. . .)

The situation was made more complicated by the fact that Mr. Gold, on his side, was under criticism from his own Marxist camp. He had just published and had been having considerable success with his book about the New York East Side, *Jews Without Money*, and the Communist critics were scolding him for having made this a volume of personal memories that centered around an individual, the official theory being that, in a Communist work of art, there ought not to be a protagonist, since the subject should be always the group. (. . .)

This whole controversy, in short, took place in an atmosphere of intellectual confusion—an atmosphere which has not yet cleared up. The results seem to have been that Michael Gold has taken to writing for the *New Masses* little Communist Sunday-school stories, in which the role of a proletarian hero is subordinated with effort and imperfect success to the conflicts of a social group; while Thornton Wilder, not unmoved, apparently, by the reproach of neglecting America, has brought out a volume of little plays several of which— and they are quite good—deal with American subjects, one of them transferring the Christian motif so obnoxious to his Marxist critics from the Greek island of *The Woman of Andros* to Trenton, New Jersey . . .

—Edmund Wilson, *The Shores of Light*, (New York: Farrar, Straus and Young, Inc., 1952): pp. 500-503, 534-539.

TYRONE GUTHRIE ON WILDER AT SEVENTY

[Tyrone Guthrie was an English actor (also known as Tyrone Power) who was knighted for services to the theatre in 1961. While serving as a judge at a drama competition in Scotland he met Wilder, then thirty. Impressed by the playwright's originality, he followed Wilder's career and offers this view of the man years later.]

Thornton Wilder the man? A compactly built person of nearly 70, he is exceptionally uninterested in his appearance and usually looks as if he had just got off a railway coach in which he has traveled for a week.

Like most human beings he is composed of such contradictory traits as would make a character in a play or a novel seem wildly unconvincing. He is probably the world's foremost authority on Lope De Vega; he knows more of history than most history professors; he can talk philosophy with philosophers, painting with painters, music with musicians. There seems to be no book which he has not only read but remembered in vivid detail.

Yet this is no secluded bookworm; it is a wildly gregarious old gossip who likes nothing so much as rushing from party to party. Colorado to Colombo, Stockholm to Buenos Aires, by plane, by train, by boat; from salon to saloon, from ritzy hotels to dockside pubs, talking, talking, talking, talking.

His talk is a low-pitched, incredibly rapid toccata with a flurried counterpoint of gesture. The bony rather square hands endlessly squirm and twiddle and poke holes in the air; and what a second ago was gossip and nonsense has suddenly turned into an immensely vivacious lecture on Plato, or Italian opera in the eighteenth century, or the influence of Joyce and Gertrude Stein, for both of whom he has an admiration which is at once passionate and rational. He is as idiotically stage-struck as a school-girl who has just come back from her first matinee; and at the same time can view the whole theatrical melee, including his own work, with a judge's impartiality and Olympian calm.

He has known almost every celebrated author, artist, musician, actor or intellectual of the day; and he enjoys to fling their names into the torrent, the maelstrom, of his conversation: "As Freud said to me in Vienna . . . I told the President of Harvard . . . When I was in Chicago with Texas Guinan . . . The Pope whispered in strict confidence . . ., Woollcott and I in Venice. . . ."

But this is no snob; and there is a stillness at the center of the maelstrom. At the end of a conversation in which Wilder seems never to have drawn breath, he will have a shrewd and tolerant and comprehensive impression of the interlocutor.

I treasure particularly happy memories of him at Stratford, Ontario, where he has been a sort of Honorary Fellow of the Shakespearean Company, attending rehearsals, buzzing like a bee in the actors' canteen, splashing dye onto costumes for plague-stricken Thebans, sitting up far into the night at parties, cross-legged on the floor among the youngsters of the company listening to them with grave attention, drawing them out and pumping them full of philosophy, psychology, religion, gossip, jokes, and just plain, practical horse-sense.

—Tyrone Guthrie, "The World of Thornton Wilder," *The Modern American Theatre*, ed. Alvin B. Kernan (Englewood Cliffs, New Jersey: Prentice-Hall, Inc., 1967): pp.50-51.

MALCOLM COWLEY ON WILDER AND HIS CONTEMPORARIES

[Malcolm Cowley was a prominent writer, editor, literary critic, poet, and translator. He is best known for editing The *Portable Faulkner* (1946). In this extract, Cowley discusses possible explanations for the difficulty of placing Wilder among his contemporaries.]

Most of the other novelists born at the turn of the century had a geographical starting point. . . . (. . .)

One thinks of Hemingway's Michigan woods, of Faulkner's county in Mississippi, of Wolfe's North Carolina mountains. (. . .)

With this generation a strong sense of place re-entered American writing for almost the first time since Hawthorne and Thoreau. (. . .)

(Wilder too is a great traveler, but he never had this sense of being exiled or expatriated, perhaps because there is no one place that he regarded as home. (. . .)

Today he is a little more of a New Englander, but chiefly he is an American whose home is wherever he opens one of his bound ledgers, uncaps a fountain pen, and begins writing about people anywhere.) (. . .)

There is a still more fundamental difference between his work and that of his contemporaries. The others write novels about a social group—sometimes a small group, as in "Tender Is the Night," sometimes a very large one, as in "U.S.A."—or they write about an individual in revolt against the group, as in "A Farewell to Arms."

The central relationship with which they deal is between the many and the one. Very often—to borrow a pair of terms from David Riesman—their theme is the defeat of an inner-directed hero by an other-directed society. They feel that the society and its standards must be carefully portrayed, and these writers are all, to some extent, novelists of manners. Wilder, on the other hand, is a novelist of morals.

Manners and morals are terms that overlap, sometimes confusingly, but here I am trying to use the two words in senses that are easier to distinguish. Manners would be the standards of conduct that prevail in a group, large or small, and hence they would change from group to group and year to year. Morals would be defined as the standards that determine the relations of individuals with other individuals, one with one—a child with each of its parents, a husband with his wife, a rich man with a poor man (not *the* rich with *the* poor)—and also the relations of any man with himself, his destiny, and his God. They are answers found by individuals to the old problems of faith, hope, love or charity, art, duty, submission to one's fate . . . and hence they are relatively universal: they can be illustrated from the lives of any individuals, in any place, at any time since the beginning of time.

The characters in Wilder's novels and plays are looking for such answers; his work is not often concerned with the behavior of groups. An outstanding exception might be his play "Our Town," in which the Stage Manager speaks with the voice of the community. But the community hasn't much to say about itself and won't admit to having local color; it might be any town, a fact that helps to explain the success of the play in towns all over this country, and other countries. The events it sets forth are coming of age, falling in love, getting married, and dying; in other words, they are not truly events, but rather examples of a universal pattern in human lives; and they are not greatly affected by the special manners of this one community.

—Malcolm Cowley, "The Man Who Abolished Time," *Critical Essays on Thornton Wilder*, ed. Martin Blank (New York: G. K .Hall & Co., 1956): pp. 32-38.

[Wilder's fascination with endless numbers and vast spaces is evident throughout his work. In this extract he is speaking about James Joyce but could as well be speaking about his own vision, particularly as it is enacted in *Our Town*.]

Now in the 20th Century, we all have something of the mind of an archaeologist. The other centuries knew that many people had lived and died a long while ago, and they knew there were many people living on the earth. But the invention of the printing press (its consequences are still unfolding) had made these realizations far more actual. Now everybody knows them, not as something you learn in school and recite to one another, but "in their bones"—that millions and billions have lived and died, and that probably billions and billions (let us not despair of the human race) will live and die. The extent of this enlarged realization alters the whole view of life.

You have lost some husband, brother, or parent in the war. Your grief is very real to you. Yet now we know as never before that a great many died in this war and in the wars of Carthage and Troy and Ur, and in the Thirty Years War—what end is there to any human thing in which you are not also companion to billions? It does not diminish your grief but it orients it to a larger field of reference.

This shift in outlook brings two results. We are less interested in the anecdote, in the "plot," Mr. So-and-so met the attractive Miss So-and-so. We wish them well; but the mere account of their progress no longer arrests us in the same way. (. . .)

The second result is an urgent search for the validity of individual experience. Though I realize that my joy or my grief is but "one" in the ocean of human life, nevertheless it has its reality. I know that the existential thing pouring up in me, my joy or my fear, is a real thing and yet that the intensity with which I feel it can be called absurd. It is absurd to claim that "I," in the vast reaches of time and place and repetition, is worth an assertion. This problem drove man back into a journey of self-examination. What is my "I"? What is the reality of my "I"? That's where the New Psychology came in.

Now Joyce is the great novelist of these two things. He is the novelist who has most succeeded in placing man in an immense field of reference, among all the people who have lived and died, in all the periods of time, all the geography of the world, all the races, all the catastrophes of history. And he is also the one who has most dramatically engaged in a search for the validity of the individual as an absolute.

—Thornton Wilder, "Joyce and the Modern Novel," *A James Joyce Miscellany*, ed. Marvin Magalaner (New York: The James Joyce Society, 1957): pp. 14-15.

REX BURBANK ON WILDER'S ESSENTIAL CONDITIONS FOR THE THEATRE

[Rex Burbank has taught English at San Jose State University in California since 1959. He has written on Sherwood Anderson and edited an anthology of American literature. In this extract, Burbank assembles and discusses Wilder's main views on drama.]

Wilder felt he could achieve in the drama what he had been trying to do in the novel without complete satisfaction to himself: eliminate the author from the narrative scene and allow the characters to reveal themselves by means of (1) "highly characteristic utterances, (2) concrete occasions in which character defines itself under action, and (3) a conscious preparation of the text whereby the actor may build upon the suggestions in the role according to his own abilities." The author provides some signs of individuality for the actor to go by, but he leaves much of the individual interpretation to the actor and concentrates his efforts upon the achievement of the general idea. The presentation is, therefore, more objective than in the novel because the "dogmatic assertions" of the omniscient novelist about his characters are eliminated. The result is that the stage can do a better job of combining the particular and the universal truth. (. . .)

[T]he theatre is addressed to the group mind, it is a kind of ritual or festival in which the audience is an indispensable part of the production. Without an audience a play would "fall to pieces and absurdity," for the excitement of pretending requires a throng. (. . .)

Wilder's third "condition"—that the theatre is a "world of pretense"—was his refutation in principle of "slice-of-life" realism.

He contended that, since the theatre is a world of pretense straining toward a general truth, scenery and sets that tie the action to a specific time and place and are intended to effect a fourth-wall realism tend to deprive the audience of its imaginative participation and require it to accept as real what it knows is not. He cited the great drama of Greece and China and of Racine and Corneille as evidence that scenery and sets are not necessary to "reality," which Wilder distinguished from the verisimilitude of realism. In this, of course, he was supported by Aristotle, who placed scenery last in the hierarchy of parts of a play, and by the Chinese, whose classic drama had only placards to identify the scenery. (. . .)

At its best the stage-play was a kind of religious ceremony in which the audience contemplated the ritual demonstration of the human condition and of the relationship of the individual to nature, to humanity, and to the cosmos. (. . .)

. . . he expressed regret that the great religious experience felt by Greek audiences is missing from the contemporary stage. The theatre, he said, "has lost one of its most powerful effects—the shudder and awe induced by the presence of the numinous, by the *tremendum* of religious experience. . . ." While Apollo was not in Oedipus, Wilder maintained that his presence was felt and that his will was the real subject of the play. The present age is not one in which a religious shudder and awe is likely to be felt as the Greek audiences felt it, but *Our Town* and *The Skin of Our Teeth* are attempts to recover for modern audiences the feeling that there is a meaningful relationship between the individual and nature, and mankind and the universe, and to restore to life those elements of mystery and love that are the basis for the affirmation of a higher presence.

> —Rex Burbank, *Thornton Wilder*, (Boston: Twayne Publishers, 1961): 73-75.

EDMUND FULLER ON WILDER'S UNIQUE QUALITIES

[Edmund Fuller is an American literary critic and historian. He wrote *Books With Men Behind Them* (1962). In this extract Fuller discusses aspects of Wilder's literary sensibility that are uncommon and undervalued.]

Wilder is unique among modern American novelists for possessing in the highest degree certain qualities currently undervalued and hence desperately needed among us. No one of his countrymen rests his work upon such an understructure of broad scholarship, cultivation and passion for the beauty and integrity of the English language. This equipment, rare in our time, gives tone to his work, especially the novels, and yet brings with it no taint of pedantry. To find work equally rich in allusion and grounded in humane learning, we must turn to English-born Aldous Huxley, although Wilder employs these attributes even more gracefully and unobtrusively than he. In a period when literary honors are bestowed often upon the craftless, the semiliterate and uncultivated, and in which the Yahoo has become hero, we need to recall that we have Wilder working among us. He helps to redeem the time.

He is notable for his versatility. Although he is not the only man writing both the novel and the play, no one else has written both at such a level of excellence, in such a marked diversity of modes, or in such form-renewing and form-extending ways as mark his work in the two media.

Wilder is a conspicuous exception to the common generalization that American writers tend to be youthful, writing of and from youth and immaturity, failing to mature in art as they age in years. He juxtaposes his always mature vision of life and character to our predominantly adolescent literature, while his range is greater than that of those established men who are most nearly his peers. There is an immense spread between the sophistication of *The Cabala* and the homely simplicity of *Our Town*, and Wilder is comfortably at home in both.

He is neither compulsive in his choice of material and method nor conditioned by some warped piping from a private clinical world. His view of life and behavior is broadly encompassing and humanely compassionate in the only true compassion, which is blended of sympathetic perception and clearly defined values.

He has the highest development and conscious control of style—having no close rival among Americans in this respect.

—Edmund Fuller, "The Notations of the Heart," *Critical Essays on Thornton Wilder*, ed. Martin Blank (New York: G.K. Hall 1956): pp. 39-40.

Mrs. Lyndon B. Johnson on Thornton Wilder's Contributions

[Mrs. Johnson praised Wilder at a ceremony on May 4, 1965, in the White House that was held in honor of his receiving the National Book Committee's first Medal for Literature.]

You have made the commonplaces of living yield the gaiety, the wonder, and the vault of the human adventure. . . . You have written with an understanding, affectionate rapport with your subjects which to me is the hallmark of genuine literature. . . .

—Mrs. Lyndon B. Johnson, included in "The World of Thornton Wilder." *Harper's Magazine* 230 (June,1965): p. 78.

Hermine I. Popper on the Universe of Thornton Wilder

[Hermine I. Popper has been managing editor of *Theatre Arts* and written film criticism. She met Wilder in childhood and comments from the perspective of having known him through the span of his life.]

Whether the Russians or the Americans finally win the race to the moon, they may find that someone has landed there before them—a graying, full-chested man with a military back and the face of an animated owl, striding briskly along in his own cloud of dust, cultivating solitude. If so they should not be surprised; for Thornton Wilder, more than any other American writer of the present century, has made his home in the universe. By experience, talent, and temperamental necessity, he has created a world beyond time and space, and he moves through it with the easy familiarity that the earthbound reserve for the Main Streets of childhood. (. . .)

"An artist is one," he wrote while still a very young man, "who knows how life should be lived at its best and is always aware of how badly he is doing it." That Wilder remains aware of this dilemma some forty years later, and has never given up the effort to stretch the recalcitrant limits of his consciousness, is part of what draws the reader back to his novels, and audiences, year after year, to his plays. (. . .)

Since the Depression, the center of literary preoccupation has shifted from economic to psychological determinism. In this context, Wilder, by maintaining that individual decision is essentially a matter of moral judgment rather than psychological necessity, still stands apart from the throng. Not that he is ignorant of Freudian concepts—indeed he had several long talks with Freud in the 'thirties and 'forties that should some day be a lively part of the record. But the understanding remains intellectual; he does not operate naturally from their premises. Thus, in the past twenty years, when both the predominant writers and the most influential critics have been shaping their images of life by moving, so to speak, from themselves as center out toward the universe, Wilder works from the universe in toward the self. (. . .)

"In life and in literature," Wilder wrote in his foreword to *The Angel That Troubled the Waters*, "mere sincerity is not sufficient, and in both realms the greater the capacity the longer the awkward age." Wilder was sixty-eight in April—"a hermit again," he wrote me not long ago, working in some deserted spa on his latest novel, which is well on the way to completion. In light of his years and the grace of his accomplishments, it may seem curious to apply to him now his own youthful phrase. Yet the awkward age is the time when more ordinary men address themselves once and for all to that most essential of human projects: to reconcile their hope for the good with their knowledge of the possible. It is a stage that Wilder, fortunately, has never outgrown.

—Hermine I. Popper, "The Universe of Thornton Wilder." *Harper's Magazine* 230, (June,1965): pp.72-73, 77, 81.

ROBERT W. CORRIGAN ON TRAGIC FEATURES OF WILDER'S VISION

[Robert W. Corrigan taught English and theatre at several institutions before becoming dean of the School of Fine

When we examine the nature of Wilder's humanistic affirmation,
what do we discover? His plays celebrate human love, the worth and
dignity of man, the values of the ordinary, and the eternity of human
values. From the little boy in Wilder's first play who says: "I am not
afraid of life. I will astonish it!" to Dolly Levi and her cohorts in
adventure in *The Matchmaker*, Wilder has always been on the side
of life and life is seen to be most directly affirmed through love.
Love, then, is his most persistent theme and it has been for him an
inexhaustible subject. Of its worth he is convinced, but it is
interesting to note that Wilder has never been able to make any
commitments as to the reasons for its worth. Wilder can deal with
life and love directly and concretely; but when he moves to the edges
of life, the focus becomes less sharp. . . .
    . . . Wilder never deals adequately with Death's own meaning. (. . .)

But although Wilder can assert meaning to life, the meaning is
almost in the assertion itself and this is not a very comfortable
position to be in. One gets the feeling that Wilder has to keep saying
it to make sure that it is true. The danger of this position is that it
lacks the necessary polarity and tension for full meaning. This in
itself keeps Wilder from being a religious dramatist. (. . .)

Wilder has not been interested in psychology and has never used
psychological techniques to solve the "modernists'" problems in the
theatre. This accounts, I think, for his great influence on the
Continental avant-garde dramatists who are rebelling against our
psychologically oriented theatre. Wilder sought to achieve the sense
of an ultimate perspective by immaterializing the sense of dramatic
place on stage. The bare stage of *Our Town* with its chairs, tables,
and ladders, together with the Stage Manager's bald exposition, are
all that he uses to create the town. The same is true of *The Skin of
Our Teeth*; you never really know where the Antrobuses live, nor
when. This is his second dominant technique; by destroying the
illusion of time, Wilder achieves the effect of any time, all time, each

time. But this is risky business, for without the backdrop of an ultimate perspective to inform a play's action, it can very easily become sentimental or satirical, or even pretentious. Wilder at his best keeps this from happening, but his only weapons are wit and irony.

—Robert W. Corrigan, *The Theatre in Search of a Fix*, (New York: Dell Publishing Co. Inc., 1973): pp. 241, 243-244, 245.

PLOT SUMMARY OF

Our Town

It is generally acknowledged that *Our Town* is performed somewhere in the world every single day. It has wide appeal, many opportunities for minimally skilled actors, plain speech, and requires barely more than a stage to produce. In an October 1937 letter to Gertrude Stein, Wilder wrote, "I am writing the most beautiful little play you can imagine." Although the play won for Wilder his second Pulitzer (1938), it encountered difficulties getting to the theatre; and, once there, of being received the way Wilder intended. He feared that the play's apparent simplicity would lead to charges of sentimentality. The first producer-director, Jed Harris, was highly enthusiastic about the play, but, wishing to make it "more entertaining," suggested changes that undermined Wilder's purposes. In his Preface to *Three Plays* (1957), the playwright was explicit:

> *Our Town* is not offered as a picture of life in a New Hampshire village; or as a speculation about…life after death.…It is an attempt to find a value above all price for the smallest events in our daily life. I have made the claim as preposterous as possible, for I have set the village against the largest dimensions of time and place.…Emily's joys and griefs,…—what are they when we consider all the billions of girls who have lived, …are living, …will live? (p.xii)

Such visionary purposes as well as his intentions to change both theme and stagecraft of American drama put Wilder in the company of his writer contemporaries such as Hemingway and Fitzgerald, who were expatriating themselves in Paris, and Faulkner, who was portraying the survival of love and honor in the racist American landscape. The author of *Our Town*, however, stands out with his more explicit (though not easy) optimism toward human and specifically American life. Early audiences, particularly in Boston, where the governor's wife walked out early saying the play was "too sad," came slowly to recognize the depth of Wilder's celebration of life, and eventually the play became a Broadway hit and a film in 1942. As recorded in G.A. Harrison's study of Wilder, *The*

Enthusiast (1983), actors from the numerous USO performances in Europe at the close of WWII recalled the "tense, rapt, even desperate looks" on the homesick faces of the GIs in the audience (p.188). *Our Town* is now regarded as a "classic" of American literature.

The play covers the years 1901-1913 and Act One is a single day, May 7, 1901, from dawn to dark in a fictional but representative small New England town. Commonplace and universal human activities are noted throughout the day: people sleep at night; get up with the sun; coexist with animals; separate themselves ("Canucks," "Polish Town,"); raise their own food; organize into separate functions and spiritual allegiances; educate themselves; feel obliviously possessive ("our mountain"); hold superstitions (Joe's knee); are born, get sick, worry, wonder, play games, argue, misbehave, gossip, get married; connect with the past, speculate about the future, and die. All five senses are included: scent of heliotrope, sound of choir, taste of coffee, sight of the moon, touch of green beans. Nothing about the day startles, and Wilder, speaking through the Stage Manager, insists explicitly on the ordinariness of the town and its inhabitants—both living and dead. The overlapping lives of two families—the Gibbs and the Webbs—is the main focus, but others' lives count as well, creating a web of life repeatable anytime and anywhere.

Three features of Act One signal that the play is more than what it seems. The first is the bare stage, one of Wilder's best-known innovations and essential to the conditions he developed for the theatre. Wilder believed that the theatre was the best art form for presenting the experience of being human. Realistic details of scenery and character bound the play to a particular time and place permitting the audience to distance itself from the action and outcomes. One could be moved by events but dismiss them as happening in the past to a character unlike oneself. Wilder believed that drama required collaboration among players including audience members who, facing a bare stage, restage the events in their own imaginations. The result is that unlike a novel with a single narrator recording actions in the past, a play is a perpetual enactment of the present.

The second feature is the Stage Manager, functioning like the

Chorus in Greek drama. His commentary reminds the audience that the theatre is based on pretense, and he can call attention to things not explicitly featured but necessary for a full view of life. He includes the dead in the cemetery, summons Editor Webb for a sociological account of the town and Professor Willard for details of geography, latitude and longitude. His hesitation about marriage as an institution and speculation about Simon Stimson's troubles show that the play does not ignore the recurring phenomenon of things going wrong, but neither of these are the point of the play. The Stage Manager points out the obvious ("This is the way we were: in our growing up and in our marrying and in our living and in our dying.") in a way that permits the audience to view life in a way not obvious.

The Stage Manager is also responsible for the third unusual feature: his presence mixes past, present, and future—creating simultaneous timeliness and timelessness. An early sentence ("First automobile's going to come along in about five years—belonged to Banker Cartwright, our richest citizen…lives in the big white house up on the hill.") contains past, present, and future tenses.

Wilder was captivated by numbers and the vastness of time and space. The density of human activity on his stage is juxtaposed against the wide and empty sky brought on by the characters' awareness of moonlight and the stars. The characters are etched with few lines in this play but there are, nonetheless, interesting variations of response. George barely notices the moon, so preoccupied is he in figuring out his math homework. Mrs. Gibbs has an entirely unmystical view of the moonlight—calling it a sign of "good potato weather"—but she stops to stare at it in silence. And Emily is distracted by the "terribleness" of the moon, responsive both to its hint of romantic aspiring and fearful nonhuman void. All these responses are legitimate and bring to the play the mysterious connection between the infinity of space and the apparent insignificance of each individual life. In an interview in the *Herald Tribune* (February 15, 1938) Wilder said that his play asks, "What is the relation between the countless 'unimportant' details of our daily life…and the great perspectives of time, social history, and recurrent religious ideas?" At the end of Act One, Rebecca's astonishment with the address on Jane's letter, which moves from town to hemisphere to Mind of God, reminds the audience that the connection between the most ordinary setting and the infinite cosmos is direct and reliable, even though incomprehensible.

The Stage Manager calls Act Two Love and Marriage, as Act One is Daily Life. After a retrospective scene in which George and Emily have a discussion about the possibility of being perfect (an issue Wilder thought a uniquely American obsession and one that reflected his interest in the Dualist view of human nature) they acknowledge that they are in love and the play moves three years ahead to July 7, 1904, their wedding day. Traditions of marriage—both silly and somber—are enacted. The sudden fearfulness that comes separately and unexpectedly to Emily and George just before their ceremony of union makes especially poignant the passing of time from the security of childhood to the responsibility of adulthood. The "presence" of the ancestors in the church and the anticipation of children from this union work to remind the audience that it is life itself being celebrated with yet another attempt of nature to produce a perfect human life.

Act Three takes place nine years later at the cemetery service for Emily who has died in childbirth and now joins the ranks of the deceased with their varying degrees of attachment to the earthly life. This innovative and startling use of the deceased on stage heightens audience awareness of their own lives. But death itself is not the riveting effect of the play; rather it is Emily's knowledge (which death enables) of the absence of awareness in the living that Wilder wishes to dramatize. The newly dead are given a choice to return to their earthly life. Warned that even an ordinary day will be too much to absorb, Emily passes over the day of falling in love with George and their wedding day together and chooses instead to relive the first part of her twelfth birthday. Mutely watching herself and her mother move through the events of waking up and eating breakfast on an ordinary morning and the ritual of gift-giving on that particular morning, Emily is overcome by the scene of human blindness. She pleads with her mother: ". . . just look at me one minute as though you really saw me . . . . just for a moment now we're all together . . . . *Let's look at one another.*" The desperate sadness that accompanies Emily's realization—that preoccupation with daily concerns obstructs for the living an understanding of the transient nature of life—becomes intolerable and she asks to return to the dead.

Wilder avoids sentimentality with Emily's refusal to mourn despite her reluctance to leave the living and also by her lament for not having lived properly herself. Moreover, her "Good-by, World" speech leaves the burden of awareness with the living in the audience who must each take responsibility for the measure of meaning the play has engendered. Suddenly, comforting mundane things like breakfast with Mama can be transformed into terrible burdens of guilt for not being sufficiently treasured. And the sense of unsurpassable security—exemplified by family life in Grover's Corners and George's faith that experts stay up all night guarding the human race against calamitous collisions in space—gives way to a terrifying insight that there is something rather than nothing and that most human beings go about their lives with minimal awareness of this astonishing fact.

After a 1969 production of *Our Town* in Harlem, a young girl in the audience stated in a later classroom discussion that the play seemed as alien to her as outer space. Emily and George reminded her of no one she knew and their plans and concerns were unrecognizable. "Irrelevant"—that infamous and ubiquitous charge—was her judgment and justification for dismissing the play. Since Wilder enthusiastically acted in his own plays, it is easy to imagine him leading his own discussions about them. He had little personal familiarity with life on urban streets amidst desperate poverty, but he was not without compassion. The anguish of Jewish refugees fleeing Nazi brutality moved him to action, and early memories of the famine in China had left a lasting impression. There is nothing known about Wilder's views that would have made it difficult for him to acknowledge the stark differences separating the calm and safe walkways of rural villages from the fearsome and chaotic streets of Harlem. In a classroom of contemporary students, however, Wilder might have dared to make the brazen claim that poverty and luxury are themselves irrelevant in the face of life itself. His purpose was to dramatize a fundamental phenomenon relevant in places of deprivation and extravagance alike with insight as potentially life-altering in both. Wilder gives Emily double vision and invites his audience to watch what happens. What she learns is that self-preoccupation gets in the way of living, makes us insensible to life until it is too late. Another way to say this is that from Emily's perspective the living are also dead. Wilder believed his purpose as a playwright was to dramatize insights of this magnitude. The moments of awareness Wilder sought for audiences of *Our Town* were reminders of the "ties that bind" human beings to each other and invitations to regard these ties as having more importance than the differences that separate us.

Our Town

THE GIBBS FAMILY

Doc Gibbs, father of George and Rebecca and wife of Julia, is the town's all-purpose doctor who delivers twins in Act I and is generally knowledgeable about the knees, heart, and stomach upsets of all the townsfolk. He performs the typical tasks of father and husband—overseeing the children's allowances and proper development, and hovering impatiently until his wife returns from choir practice. Emotionally vulnerable on his son's wedding day, he reveals that having a son has sometimes been "terrifying" and that years ago he feared (with no reason) that he and his wife would run out of things to say to each other. Doc Gibbs aspirations extend as far as visiting Civil War battlegrounds every other year, worried that a trip to Europe might make him discontented with his little hometown.

Julia Gibbs would "rather have [her] children healthy than bright" and hovers, mother hen-like, over them. Her secret aspiration is to "see Paris, France" which she could afford by selling her old highboy to an antique dealer from Boston, but the money goes instead years later to support George and Emily's new farm. On her son's wedding day after fretting about her boy's youthfulness and announcing "weddings are perfectly awful things," she makes for her husband a special breakfast of French toast. Among those living without full awareness, Julia Gibbs is nonetheless aware enough to stop to smell the heliotrope in the moonlight.

George Gibbs struggles with his studies and shines on his baseball team. He is immune to the power of moonlight but gets excited about being a good farmer although not excited enough to attend college to learn more. He represents the continuity of the land and family farming by taking on his uncle's old farm. George is left with a full burden of grief and the task of being a single father.

Rebecca Gibbs worries about her clothes and is a little stingy with her allowance money. She gets carried away one night contemplating the address on an envelope that puts her little town right into the cosmos and the unimaginable Mind of God, yet gets delivered anyway.

THE WEBB FAMILY

Editor Webb keeps track of social arrangements and political allegiances including the small percentage of townspeople who are "indifferent." For pastimes Mr. Webb unapologetically reports a lot of simple and passive watching—of birds, change of seasons, sun risings and settings. He is aware of cultural achievements but cannot come up with anything outstanding, listing for musical achievement: school girls reluctantly playing the piano for Commencement, and the traditional rendering of Handel's "Largo" in one of the churches. Despite his relatively impressive education, Editor Webb lacks knowledge of, but not concern for, the social issues of injustice and inequality, and seems unable to imagine any proposals to adequately deal with these ancient human dilemmas. He adores his daughter Emily and teases her about putting on airs and then feigns surprise at getting "a kiss from such a great lady."

Myrtle Webb takes no nonsense from her children. She responds to Emily's claims of being the brightest girl in the class with an admonishment to eat her breakfast. When Emily worries about being pretty she gives no satisfaction to her daughter, replying that she is "pretty enough for all normal purposes" when Emily really wants to be told she is the most beautiful girl in the world. Mrs. Webb reveals the never-quite-submerged female vanity when she insists that she herself was in fact the prettiest girl in her day, but these spats between herself and Emily are essentially harmless. Mrs. Webb suffers the double grief of losing both children before they have had a full life.

Emily Webb is proud of her intellectual abilities, claiming to be both "healthy" and "bright" at the same time. She has aspirations both romantic and imaginative, but none that will draw her away from her hometown and George. Emily is the only complex character in *Our Town*, acquiring through death a capacity for double vision—living and watching herself living—that engenders a profound love and awareness of life which she imparts to the audience to contemplate.

Wally Webb, in his sister's shadow, says he's smart too "when [he's] looking at [his] stamp collection." Having died very young on a camping trip in the mountains, Wally is among the deceased when Emily arrives at the cemetery.

The **Stage Manager**, providing, as he does, unity for the play, lacks distinctive characteristics but he does exhibit common human virtues and features (curiosity, wit, sympathy, speculative intelligence, and—that saving quality—irony) as well as the nonhuman capacity to summon the past and foretell the future.

CRITICAL VIEWS ON

Our Town

MARY MCCARTHY ON USING DECEASED CHARACTERS ON STAGE

[Mary McCarthy was a prominent American intellectual particularly known for her outspoken views against hypocrisy. She taught English at Sarah Lawrence College and the University of London. She is best known for her novel *The Group* (1963) and memoir *Memories of a Catholic Girlhood* (1957). She was also an editor of *The Partisan Review.* In this extract she comments on Wilder's innovative use of the deceased on stage as characters.]

Mr. Wilder's fourth innovation is the most striking. In order to dramatize his feelings about life he has literally raised the dead. At the opening of the third act a group of people are discovered sitting in rows on one side of the stage; some of the faces are familiar, some are new. They are speaking quite naturally and calmly, and it is not until one has listened to them for some minutes that one realizes that this is the cemetery and these are the dead. A young woman whom we have seen grow up and marry the boy next door has died in childbirth; a small, shabby funeral procession is bringing her to join her relatives and neighbors. Only when she is actually buried does the play proper begin. She has not yet reached the serenity of the long dead, and she yearns to return to the world. With the permission of the stage manager and against the advice of the dead, she goes back—to a birthday of her childhood. Hardly a fraction of that day has passed, however, before she retreats gratefully to the cemetery, for she has perceived that the tragedy of life lies in the fragmentary and imperfect awareness of the living.

Mr. Wilder's play is, in a sense, a refutation of its own thesis. *Our Town* is purely and simply an act of awareness, a demonstration of the fact that in a work of art, at least, experience *can* be arrested, imprisoned, and vicariously felt. The perspective of death, which Mr. Wilder has chosen, gives an extra poignancy and intensity of the small-town life whose essence he is trying so urgently to communicate. The little boy delivering papers, for example, becomes more touching, more meaningful and important, when Mr. Craven announces casually that he is going to be killed in the War. The boy's morning round, for the spectator, is transfigured into an absorbing ritual; the unconsciousness of the character has heightened the consciousness of the audience. The perspective is, to be sure, hazardous: it invites bathos and sententiousness. Yet Mr. Wilder has used it honorably. He forbids the spectator to dote on that town of the past. He is concerned only with saying: this is how it was, though then we did not know it. Now and then, of course, his memory fails him, for young love was never so baldly and tritely gauche as his scene in the soda fountain suggests. This is, however, a deficiency of imagination, not an error of taste; and except in the third act, where the dead give some rather imprecise and inapposite definitions of the nature of the after-life, the play keeps its balance beautifully. In this feat of equilibrium Mr. Wilder has had the complete cooperation of Mr. Craven, the serene, inexorable matter-of-factness of whose performance acts as a discipline upon the audience. Mr. Craven makes on quite definitely homesick, but pulls one up sharp if one begins to blubber about it.

—Mary McCarthy, "Theatre Chronicle," *The Partisan Review* IV (April,1938): pp. 55-56.

A.R. Fulton on Expressionistic Influences

[A.R. Fuller taught English at Purdue University. He is known for his writing on movies and the transition from silent films to television. In this extract, he discusses Wilder's use of techniques from the German Expressionists to heighten emotion in his productions.]

In negating the three walls *Our Town* manifests expressionism. The scenery, too, in this play is expressionistic—the chairs and tables for the interior of the houses and the trellises for the exteriors, the stepladders for second floors, the plank supported by chair backs for ironing board as well as soda fountain, chairs for graves and for pews in the church, and even the screen of umbrellas from behind which Emily appears in the graveyard scene. The lack of conventional scenery expresses one of the most important media of all the stage itself. The play manifests expressionism not only in negating the three walls but in projecting the fourth wall. The curtain is up and the house lights are on as the action begins. The Stage Manager, pipe in mouth, "leaning against the right proscenium pillar watches the late arrivals in the audience." Steps leading down from the stage to the orchestra provide an exit through the auditorium. Theatrical illusion is also broken down when lines are spoken by the Woman in the Balcony, the Tall Man at Back of Auditorium, and the Lady in a Box. The church choir sings in the orchestra pit. The stage is projected, too, in the monologues of the Stage Manager, Editor Webb, and Professor Willard. In fact the entire play might be considered a monologue—the monologue of the Stage Manager, illustrated by the acting of the other characters and even by the Stage Manager himself. (. . .)

Our Town, its author has declared, "sprang from a deep admiration for those little white towns in the hills and from a deep devotion to the theatre." This is significant, because it testifies to Mr. Wilder's concern not only with the meaning of his play but with the very practical problem of how to present the meaning on the stage. *Our Town* exemplifies a proper collaboration of staging and content, of theatre and drama. Although his play is not essentially expressionistic, Mr. Wilder could not have written it if his devotion to the theatre had not implied an appreciation of the [...] expressionists, who had shown how the stage can express meaning beyond reality—meaning which cannot be expressed by realism in scenery, stage properties, and acting. (. . .)

The danger in realistic scenery is that the scenery can exist for its own sake. In *Our Town* the scenery never does. However, although it does not obtrude beyond its proper function of helping to interpret the play, it performs this function so smoothly and so simply that *Our Town* illustrates more distinctly than any other modern play one of the most significant contributions of expressionism—an harmonious collaboration of drama and theatre.

—A.R. Fulton, "Expressionism—Twenty Years After," *The Sewanee Review* 52 (July-September, 1944): pp. 411-413.

[Arthur Miller is a prominent American playwright. He is best known for his Pulitzer Prize-winning play *Death of a Salesman* (1949) and *The Crucible* (1953). In 1984 he received the JFK Lifetime Achievement Award. In this extract Miller examines different conceptualizations of family in American drama with a focus on *Our Town*.]

We recognize now that a play can be poetic without verse, and it is in this middle area that the complexities of tracing the influence of the family and social elements upon the form become more troublesome. *Our Town* by Thornton Wilder is such a play, and it is important not only for itself but because it is the progenitor of many other works.

This is a family play which deals with the traditional family figures, the father, mother, brother, sister. At the same time it uses this particular family as a prism through which is reflected the author's basic idea, his informing principle—which can be stated as the indestructibility, the everlastingness, of the family and the community, its rhythm of life, its rootedness in the essentially safe cosmos despite troubles, wracks, and seemingly disastrous, but essentially temporary, dislocations.

Technically it is not arbitrary in any detail. Instead of a family living room or a house, we are shown a bare stage on which actors set chairs, a table, a ladder to represent a staircase or an upper floor, and so on. A narrator is kept in the foreground as though to remind us that this is not so much "real life" as an abstraction of it—in other words, a stage. It is clearly a poetic rather than a realistic play. What makes it that? Well, let us first imagine what would make it more realistic.

Would a real set make it realistic? Not likely. A real set would only discomfit us by drawing attention to what would then appear to be a slightly unearthly quality about the characterizations. We should probably say, "People don't really act like that." In addition, the characterization of the whole town could not be accomplished with anything like its present vividness if the narrator were removed, as he would have to be from a realistic set, and if the entrances and exits of the environmental people, the townspeople, had to be justified with the usual motives and machinery of Realism.

The preoccupation of the entire play is quite what the title implies—the town, the society, and not primarily this particular family—and every stylistic means used is to the end that the family foreground be kept in its place, merely as a foreground for the larger context behind and around it. In my opinion, it is this larger context, the town and its enlarging, widening significance, that is the bridge to the poetic for this play. Cut out the town and you will cut out the poetry.

The play is worth examining further against the Ibsen form of Realism to which it is inevitably related if only in contrast. Unlike Ibsen, Wilder sees his characters in this play not primarily as personalities, as individuals, but as forces, and he individualizes them only enough to carry the freight, so to speak, of their roles as forces. I do not believe, for instance, that we can think of the brother in this play, or the sister or the mother, as having names other than Brother, Sister, Mother. They are not given that kind of particularity or interior life. They are characterized rather as social factors, in their roles of Brother, Sister, Mother, in *Our Town*. They are drawn, in other words, as forces to enliven and illuminate the author's symbolic vision and his theme, which is that of the family as a timeless, stable quantity which has not only survived all the turmoil of time but is, in addition, beyond the possibility of genuine destruction.

The play is important to any discussion of form because it has achieved a largeness of meaning and an abstraction of style that created that meaning, while at the same time it has moved its audiences subjectively—it has made them laugh and weep as abstract plays rarely if ever do. But it would seem to contradict my contention here. If it is true that the presentation of the family on the stage inevitably forces Realism upon the play, how did this family play manage to transcend Realism to achieve its symbolistic style?

Every form, every style, pays its price for its special advantages. The price paid by *Our Town* is psychological characterization forfeited in the cause of the symbol. I do not believe, as I have said, that the characters are identifiable in a psychological way, but only as figures in the family and social constellation, and this is not meant in criticism, but as a statement of the limits of this form. I would go further and say that it is not *necessary* for every kind of play to do every kind of thing. But if we are after ultimate reality we must make ultimate demands.

I think that had Wilder drawn his characters with a deeper configuration of detail and with a more remorseless quest for private motive and self-interest, for instance, the story as it stands now would have appeared oversentimental and even sweet. I think that if the play tested its own theme more remorselessly, the world it creates of a timeless family and a rhythm of existence beyond the disturbance of social wracks would not remain unshaken. The fact is that the juvenile delinquent is quite directly traced to the breakup of family life and, indeed, to the break in that ongoing, steady rhythm of community life which the play celebrates as indestructible.

I think, further, that the close contact which the play established with its audience was the result of its coincidence with the deep longing of the audience for such stability, a stability which in daylight out on the street does not truly exist. The great plays pursue the idea of loss and deprivation of an earlier state of bliss which the characters feel compelled to return to or to re-create. I think this play forgoes the loss and suffers thereby in its quest for reality, but that the audience supplies the sense of deprivation in its own life experience as it faces what in effect is an idyl of the past. To me, therefore, the play falls short of a form that will press into reality to the limits of reality, if only because it could not plumb the psychological interior lives of its characters and still keep its present form. It is a triumph in that it does open a way toward the dramatization of the larger truths of existence while using the common materials of life. It is a truly poetic play.

—Arthur Miller, "The Family in Modern Drama," *The Atlantic Monthly* 197 (April, 1956): pp. 38-39.

WINFIELD TOWNLEY SCOTT ON USES OF SIMPLICITY

[Winfield Townley Scott was an editor and full-time writer. He taught at Brown, Tufts, and Harvard and received several awards for his published poetry. Wilder feared his play would mistakenly be seen as sentimental and he regarded this review by Scott as the first to understand his intentions.]

The whole tone of *Our Town* is understatement. The colloquial run of the talk, its occasional dry wit, the unheroic folk, all contribute to this tone. So does the important admission that this is a play: we are not bid to suspend our disbelief in the usual way; and so does the bareboard, undecorated presentation. All is simple, modest, easy, plain. And so, in tone, the Stage Manager's revelation is utterly casual. But with it Wilder sets in countermotion to the little wheel a big wheel; and as the little one spins the little doings, the big one begins slowly—slowly—for it is time itself, weighted with birth and marriage and death, with aging and with change. This is the great thing that *Our Town* accomplishes; simultaneously we are made aware of what is momentary and what is eternal. We are involved by the Stage Manager in these presented actions and yet like him we are also apart; we are doubly spectators, having a double vision. We are not asked, as in the presentation of some philosophical concept, to perceive an abstract intellectualism. This is a play—this is art. So we are involved sensually and emotionally. Out of shirt-sleeved methods that would seem to defy all magic, and because of them not in spite of them, Wilder's play soon throttles us with its pathos; convinces and moves us so that we cannot imagine its being done in any other way; assumes a radiant beauty. And indeed we are not taken out of ourselves, we are driven deeper into ourselves. This, we say, is life: apparently monotonous, interminable, safe; really all mutable, brief, and in danger. "My," sighs the dead Mrs. Soames in Act III, "wasn't life awful—and wonderful." For what Wilder's art has reminded us is that beauty is recognizable because of change and life is meaningful because of death. (. . .)

The wit is Yankee laconic; sometimes so wry you may ask if it is wit. Noting that lights are on in the distant farmhouses while most of Grover's Corners itself is still dark at six o'clock in the morning, the Stage Manager says, "But town people sleep late." It is funny—but is it funny to the Stage Manager? We have no way of knowing that the Stage Manager does not feel that people who don't get up till six-thirty or seven are late sleepers. This is a part of the charm.

The charm does not evade the big and the ephemeral troubles of life, the tears of youth and of age, and the terminal fact of death. As *Our Town* develops, it is more and more incandescent with the charges of change and of ending. There is not in it any of the ugliness present in the small-town books I have likened it to: the violence and murder in *Tom Sawyer*, the meannesses and frustrations in *Spoon River Anthology*[5] and *Winesburg, Ohio*. Yet these, books also glow with a nostalgic beauty. True, the drunken, disappointed organist would be at home either in Masters' Spoon River or in Robinson's Tilbury Town; and in Act II, at the time of George's wedding, there is the bawdiness of the baseball players which, significantly, the Stage Manager quickly hushes.[6] Brief touches: not much. Nevertheless, I would defend *Our Town* against the instant, obvious question whether Wilder in excluding harsher facts indigenous to life has written a sentimental play, by insisting Wilder would have warped the shape of his plan by such introductions. He was out not to compose a complete small-town history nor, on the other hand, to expose a seamy-sided one; his evident purpose was to dramatize the common essentials of the lives of average people. There are other colors, no doubt more passionate, but they would have deranged this simple purpose which, as I see it, is valid and has been well served.

Notes

5. *Our Town* contains a paraphrase reference to *Spoon River Anthology*. When the Stage Manager says, nearing the beginning of Act II, "It's like what one of those Middle West poets said: You've got to love life to have life, and you've got to have life to love life . . . / It's what they call a vicious circle," he is echoing the "Lucinda Matlock" poem which ends "Degenerate sons and daughters, / Life is too strong for you— / It takes life to love Life." . . . Edgar Lee Masters (I am informed on excellent authority) convinced himself that Thornton Wilder "stole" the whole concept of *Our Town* from *Spoon River Anthology*.
6. The bawdiness is softened in revised text.

—Winfield Townley Scott, *Exiles and Fabrications*, (Garden City, New York: Doubleday& Company, Inc., 1961): pp. 83, 87-88.

[Travis Bogard was a literary critic and historian and created the dramatic art program at the University of California at Berkeley. He became director of artistic programs at the Eugene O'Neill Tao House Foundation. In this extract, Bogard discusses Wilder's methods of avoiding sentimental responses to the mundane.]

The theater is the natural home of the cliché. Stereotypes of character, situation, and belief which a novelist would be embarrassed to conceive, much less develop, come to their particular fulfillment in the theater. Only at the theater is one treated so frequently to innocent adulteries and guilt-ridden matrimonial triangles, to psychopathic villains terrorizing the incipiently courageous, to drifters questing for mothers who have betrayed them, to homespun philosophers crackling with rural wisdom, to melodramatized conflicts between dark and light, right and left, vice and virtue. Only at the theater is experience formulated in terms of repetitious stylizations of human behavior and accepted with so little effective question.

At its worst, the theatrical cliché beggars insight, heating the theater with false passion, with concepts empty of thought, and with attitudes that have been assumed for the occasion—without reference to morality or to psychology. (. . .)

A dramatist must do more than give new names to old situations. He must not merely accept them, but must search them for their human roots. He must fit them into a larger concept of his action so that they do more than thrill cheaply the emotions of the spectator. The best balance sets character as both individual and symbol, exploring in a given situation the dilemmas of the individual man and the meaning he has in a larger scheme of implication. In establishing both the immediate and the general, the cliché character and situation are often serviceable as connecting points, for they base themselves on possible human actions; at the same time, because they have been used in so many dramas, they suggest an archetypical possibility through which the largest significance of the action may be developed.(. . .)

The essential difference between *Our Town* and the bulk of American folk drama is that Wilder attempts to convince no one of his truth by insisting that what he presents is the reality itself. If his story had been developed realistically, carefully plotted, decorated so as to attempt to convince the audience that it was seeing living human beings, much of its truth would have drained from the play, and all of it would have seemed sentimental and unconvincing. But Wilder, as his earlier plays suggested he might, avoids this and with it much of the fraudulence of American folk drama. He insists that the actors are only pretending to be characters. They are stage-managed; they are in rehearsal, so to speak. Above all, they are not attempting to convince anyone of the reality of their illusionary comings and goings. They are deliberately depicted as theatrical stereotypes.

The result is that Wilder's characters become emblems of reality, not reality itself. They are there to remind audiences of familiar things in whose recognition there is pleasure and security. Like the statistics quoted in the opening sequences of the play, the things the characters do are ways of naming blessings.[1] The characters seem a little like priests, the guardians of a shrine whose rituals they only dimly comprehend. In their appointed rounds they touch familiar things and receive a kind of blessing from the act. They are secure in eternity, and what they do is a ritual enactment of realities which do not need analysis. And because they are deliberate artifices, they escape the merely sentimental. What they touch has the power of a propitiatory charm, a tribal totem, warding off any invasion of evil or doubt.

The distance provided by the artifice permits the drama to move through broken scenes, fragmentarily tracing the lives of George and Emily and their families and their neighbors. Its primary emotion is the joy of discovery and remembering the discovery of the limited world. Moving backward and forward in time and place, the scenes form, in the end, a whole and describe man's course in the timeless cycle of eternity. Even the moment of greatest agony, when Emily returns to earth and cries out that man is unaware of joy as it passes, diminishes in the free slip of time. Tears drain into the earth and memory lies light as the flesh disappears and as thought releases its hold on dead limbs.

For an audience, this is the value of the play: that it reminds men of the good underlying their hesitation, doubts and agony. It promises no salvation, but, equally, in *Our Town* no one is damned. Wilder does not deny the reality of suffering, the necessity of questing and inquiry, but he sees that all such passion and acts of will pass away in the surcease of eternity.

NOTE

1. Detailed biographical evidence is lacking in substantiation, but his plays suggest that Wilder himself touched reality as firmly and as often as he could. For instance, in *The Happy Journey to Trenton and Camden* he names a high school principal, Mr. Biedenbach, who was in fact the principal of the Berkeley (California) High School which Wilder attended. In the same play, the characters pass and comment on the Lawrenceville Academy where Wilder was teaching as he wrote the play. A sudden blurring of artifice and reality occur as if the characters were watching Wilder watching them.

> —Travis Bogard, "The Comedy of Thornton Wilder," *The Modern American Theatre*, ed. Alvin B. Kernan (Englewood Cliffs, New Jersey: Prentice-Hall, Inc., 1967): pp. 52-53, 61-62.

MALCOLM GOLDSTEIN ON EMILY'S "GOOD-BY, WORLD" SPEECH

[Malcolm Goldstein teaches English at Queens College in New York City. In addition to his book on Wilder, he has published articles on American drama. Here, he discusses Emily's speech as the culmination of the play.]

With this scene we come to a point to which Wilder always directs us: the belief that the cause of man's unhappiness is not his failure to achieve or sustain greatness, but his failure to delight in the beauty of ordinary existence. In the preface to his Three Plays, the collected edition of his major dramatic works, he writes forthrightly of this theme:

> *Our Town* is not offered as a picture of life in a New Hampshire Village; or as speculation about the conditions of life after death (that element I merely took from Dante's *Purgatory*). It is an attempt to find a value above all price for the smallest events in

our daily life.... Molière said that for the theatre all he needed was a platform and a passion or two. The climax of this play needs only five square feet of boarding and the passion to know what life means to us. (pp. xii–xiii)

The people of Grover's Corners are the sort whose effect upon the world is slight, slighter even than the effect of such a man as George Brush, since they never move away from their particular piece of the universe. For that reason they are the personages whose lives most clearly reflect the marvelousness of the unheroic.

Wilder's choice of New England for the setting strengthens the play to the extent, as we have observed, that a depiction of fundamental passions may be especially moving to an American audience if the scene itself is fundamentally and simply American. In this regard, no region qualifies so well as does the birthplace of the nation. On the other hand, nothing vital would be lost if the setting were changed to any other uncomplicated community; in 1962 *Life* illustrated the play very satisfactorily with a series of photographs of a small town in South Dakota where it had recently been performed.[6] For that matter, Rome, Lima, the Greek islands, and the American Midwest had served Wilder as backgrounds against which to project the same theme, though none had proved quite so successful as the New Hampshire village. For Wilder's purposes in the play, the uniquely indispensable characteristic of the community's populace is its colloquial speech. (. . .)

That the play is a tragedy, despite the simplicity of the dialogue, is beyond dispute, for we see the death of Emily cutting short the happiness which the young protagonists had earned by the conduct of their lives. Their distress brings the reminder that no amount of effort to achieve honor and dignity such as theirs will confer immortality. The only mitigating notion lies in Emily's urgent lament for the lost opportunity to enjoy simple pleasures. The wisest onlookers will respond to the implicit warning of her last speeches and make what use of it they can. Possibly it will function in their lives to increase their own awareness.

NOTE

6. "The Abiding Truths of '*Our Town*,'" *Life*, LIII (Sept. 7, 1962), 52–67.

—Malcolm Goldstein, *The Art of Thornton Wilder,* (Lincoln, Nebraska: University of Nebraska Press, 1965): pp. 105-107.

DONALD HABERMAN ON TIME

[Donald Haberman is a professor of English at Arizona State University. In this extract he discusses the power Wilder achieves by mixing the time tenses.]

The glimpses of future time—that is, time after the action of the play but before the time of the audience—reminders that what happens is actually time past, are more than inverse flashbacks. They represent, like the sudden return on the wedding day to George's proposal to Emily, a consistent and deliberate rearrangement of time. The logic that dominates the play has little relation to the progression of historical time, although Wilder reminds the audience that as individuals they must all finally submit to the tyranny of that historical time. Partly Wilder relies on this confusion, as with the interruption by the proposal, to prevent the ordinariness of subject matter from seeming uninteresting. More importantly, however, the interruption of events without having any of them reach a conclusion—George never really gets around to proposing to Emily—prevents them, and their place as one in a great number, from being overlooked. They are never one part of a sequence, but always stand out in their own separateness.

The reminder of time past seems to work directly in opposition to Wilder's idea of the stage's eternal now; however, as memory it moves with a logic all its own and exists as present time. He said in 1952 in a magazine article, "The American Loneliness," "Time is something we create, we call into being, not something we submit to—an order outside us."[14] By recalling past time, Wilder has, in the three acts of his play, created his own time separate from that time of the audience which ticks away each minute. He has presented in recognizable sequence birth, marriage, and death, events analogous to the cycle of life of any member of the audience. But the sequence—particularly its end in death—gives the events a special poignancy, and the events achieve a meaning beyond the sequence. Each event in the life of Emily Webb is single and unimportant, but more, each event is also part of a universe too vast to imagine. The repeated shifts in time are reminders that all parts of life's sequence are in operation for any number of people at any time. It is the force of memory that is always in the present tense. This memory, juggling all the events at once like a circus performer, keeps the action in the eternal now on stage. Wilder offers memory as the real thing, feeling that it has a greater value than the actual experience. Witnessing the past with all the advantages of hindsight but without the power to change anything dramatizes the anguish of the inadequacy of life.

NOTE

14. Thornton Wilder, "The American Loneliness," *Atlantic*, CXC (August, 1952), 68.

—Donald Haberman, *The Plays of Thornton Wilder*, (Middletown, Connecticut: Wesleyan University Press, 1967): pp. 57-58.

M.C. KUNER ON THE FUNCTION OF THE STAGE MANAGER

[M.C. Kuner is a playwright who teaches drama at Hunter College in New York City. In this extract she discusses the way Wilder uses the figure of the Stage Manager to implement aspects of his theory of drama.]

Another theory that Wilder propounded was that the action in a play "takes place in a perpetual present time. . . . Novels are written in the past tense. . . . On the stage it is always now." In addition, the novel has the advantage of an omniscient author who can tell his readers facts that the other characters do not know; on a stage everything must be presented between the characters. Wilder pointed out that the Greek Chorus performed just such a function in the theater, and he believed that the modern playwright had to find an equivalent— as he was to do in supplying the Stage Manager for *Our Town*. A play thus provided with a Stage Narrator attains a kind of timelessness, for the narrator can be part of the play's momentary action and yet be a commentator on what has happened in the past; or he can look into the future and tell the audience what he sees, for he is both enclosed in finite time and stands beyond, outside it. Finally, if he can move back and forth in time so freely, he must be aware of the repetitions of history and the ideas that flow from one century to the next, and so he becomes a transmitter of myth, legend, allegory. In such a theater the characters are analogous not to the planets, which "wander," but to the stars, which are fixed; while the background or setting, like the earth itself, moves in time.

Observing that the theater is a world of pretense, Wilder ennumerated such conventions as the playing of women's roles by men in the Greek (and Elizabethan) age; the use of metric speech, although in life people do not speak verse; the reliance on masks and other devices. And he argued that these conventions did not spring from naiveté but from the vitality of the public imagination: they provoked the audience into participating instead of having all the work done for them by the dramatist. Even more important, in Wilder's estimation, the action was thereby raised from specific to the general. (. . .)

Our Town is, therefore, the blossoming of Wilder's theories. Emily and George are types rather than individuals, outlines rather than photographs. Although the play begins in America's past (between 1901 and 1913), it deals with the future, too. For in the end, Emily, having died, comes back to visit Grover's Corners; she exists simultaneously in all three pockets of time. The Stage Manager constantly reminds us of the make-believe quality of the play by asking us to imagine this or that prop; he himself plays different roles in addition to his own; he is not limited by sex, since he takes the part of Mrs. Morgan as well as of other men in the town; and from time to time he comments on the weather or the state of the world, lectures to the audience, and interprets the actions of the characters for us. Wilder even succeeds in supplying us with ritual: the hum of activity that makes up everyday life. One might almost say that brushing one's teeth or one's hair is a ritual; Wilder picks up moments like these to affirm that all of us are bound together in one vast chain, because we all share certain common thoughts and actions.

—M.C. Kuner, Thornton Wilder: *The Bright and the Dark*, (New York: Thomas Y. Crowell Company, 1972): 125-128.

[Linda Simon teaches in the expository writing program at Harvard. In addition to her work on Wilder, she has written biographies of Alice B. Toklas and Gertrude Stein. Here she reviews a selection of reviews of *Our Town*.]

Brooks Atkinson, in the *New York Times*, called it "a beautifully evocative play." Wilder, be wrote, "has transmuted the simple events of human life into universal reverie. He has given familiar facts a deeply moving, philosophical perspective. . . . '*Our Town*' has escaped from the formal barrier of the modern theatre into the quintessence of acting, thought and speculation." The play was "one of the finest achievements of the current stage," and Wilder, who had won his fame as a writer of fiction, must now be considered an eminent dramatist. Atkinson was struck, especially, by the unique atmosphere that Thornton created. ". . . By stripping the play of everything that is not essential, Mr. Wilder has given it a profound, strange, unworldly significance. This is less the portrait of a town than the sublimation of the commonplace; and in contrast with the universe that silently swims around it, it is brimming over with compassion."[19]

Edith Isaacs, whose review appeared later in *Theatre Arts*, welcomed Thornton "to the thin ranks of our serious playwrights. . . ." He wrote, she said, "with the gift of humor, of simplicity, of moderation added to his recognized talent for story-telling and characterization." Thornton, she continued, "appears to search no deeper into character or motive than a man strolling down Main Street," yet he managed to create a story "that runs like a bright thread across the pattern of village life."[20]

But Thornton's former supporter Stark Young had reservations about the play's merits. "The prevailing tone of it is essentially literary," he thought, though he admitted that the scene where the dead sit on their graves waiting for Emily provided "a stage image that is unforgettable." The play as a whole was "a kind of factual reverie" of small-town life, but without "the bite, the unpredictable, the deep glimpse, the divine insight and the wayward taste" of Sherwood Anderson's *Winesburg, Ohio*. "All the assumption of homely effect is not so much a thing itself, the actual life and town, as something we see arise from dreams of it."[21]

Nevertheless, the play received accolades from important reviewers like John Mason Brown, who wrote that he surrendered "especially during the first act, to the spell of the beautiful and infinitely tender play. . . . Mr. Wilder's play is laid in no imaginary place," he concluded. "It becomes reality in the human heart."[22] The reviews were so positive that Harris had no trouble finding another theater—the Morosco—in which to continue the play's Broadway run. But the weekly receipts were, he reported, "on a very mediocre level." ". . . The show actually had more losing weeks than profitable weeks during its entire New York engagement. In mid-June, when the play bad been running four months, it was losing on an average of five hundred dollars a week and it was necessary to ask the cast to take a cut in salary in order to stay open at all." The play did not offer the attractions of other Broadway shows: it lacked scenery, which some thought was a way of saving money; it was not a tuneful musical; it was thought to be somewhat morose—at least according to one notable viewer. Eleanor Roosevelt saw *Our Town* and said it had "moved her and depressed her beyond words. '*Our Town*' . . . is . . . interesting and . . . original and I am glad I saw it, but I did not have a pleasant evening," she reported.[23]

And two others, of more concern to Thornton than Mrs. Roosevelt also did not enjoy the play: Thornton's mother and his sister Isabel. "You see," he explained, "'*Our Town*' inevitably means our family, too. I remember my sister asking, 'Mother, am I pretty?' and when my folks sit there and see themselves say that very thing in the show, they find it harrowing."[24]

Notes

19. February 5, 1938.
20. March 1938, 172–73.
21. *New Republic*, February 23, 1938, 74.
22. Brown, *Two on the Aisle*, 189, 193.
23. New York *Herald Tribune*, March 13, 1938.
24. Wisconsin *State Journal*, October 6, 1940.

—Linda Simon, *Thornton Wilder: His World,* (Garden City, New York: Doubleday & Company, Inc., 1979): pp.143-144.

GILBERT A. HARRISON ON *OUR TOWN* FROM PLAY TO FILM

[Gilbert A. Harrison befriended the Wilder family and
hundreds of actors, directors, and other playwrights
connected to Wilder to write his appreciative biography. In
this extract, Harrison gives an account of Wilder's relation
to Sol Lesser, who in 1939 had bought the motion picture
rights to *Our Town* and proposed changes in the plot.]

Thornton worried that if it was realistically photographed, the
wedding of Emily and George would reduce many of the
surrounding scenes to ordinariness. He pointed out that on the stage,
novelty had been supplied by the absence of scenery, by the Stage
Manager's playing the minister, by thinking-aloud passages, by the
oddity of hearing someone gabble during the ceremony, and by the
young people's moments of alarm. "You have none of these." "Now,
Sol," he wrote diplomatically,

> it's just you I'm thinking about; will you have as *interesting* a pic-
> ture as you hoped? This treatment seems to be in danger of dwin-
> dling to the conventional. And for a story that's so generalized
> that's a great danger. The play interested because every few min-
> utes there was a new bold effect in presentation-methods. For the
> movie it may be an audience-risk to be bold (thinking of the forty
> millions) but I think with this story it's a still greater risk to be
> conventional. I know you'll realize I don't mean boldness or odd-
> ity for their own sakes, but merely as the almost indispensable
> reenforcement and refreshment of a play that was never intended
> to be interesting for its story alone, or even for its background.

Hating to seem like a "vain author [who] thinks every word
sacred," Thornton nonetheless insisted that cuts in the death-and-
immortality speech harmed it; "in its present shape it reads like a
sweetness-and-light Aimee McPherson spiel." And the wedding
scene was still not fresh enough: "I don't think that realistic boys in
a realistic village would hoot and guy a friend on his way to his
wedding. That's Dead-End-Kids city life." (. . .)

Thornton did not object, however, to a major change from the
stage version—Emily's survival.

Emily should live. I've always thought so. In a movie you see the people so close to that a distant relation is established. In the theater they are halfway abstractions in an allegory; in the movie they are very concrete. So insofar as the play is a generalized allegory she dies—we die—they die; insofar as it's a Concrete Happening it's not important that she die; it's even disproportionately cruel that she die. Let her live—the idea will have been imparted anyway. But if she lives, I agree with you that after all that graveyard material the survival may seem too arbitrary and abrupt and out of relation to the Stage Manager presiding over the experience. Hence: Your first suggestion is fine. Sick-in-bed we hear her say faintly, "I want to live! I want to live." Then the whole graveyard sequence and the return to the birthday and back to the sick bed; and a louder "I want to live." This may give the impression that all the intervening material was a dream or hallucination that took place in a second of time—that is: between her second and third cries of "I want to live"—which is the right idea.

On the train from New York to New Haven for Isabel's birthday in January 1940, Thornton read the latest *Our Town* script and was dissatisfied with additional business that might get a laugh but would establish the wrong tone: "A few more stealing-donuts, dish-towel errors, four spoonfuls-of-sugar, drinking-coffee-out-of-saucers, mothers-looking-behind-sons'-ears—and the audience would be justified in believing this is one of those pictures of Quaint Hayseed Family Life."

—Gilbert A. Harrison, *The Enthusiast: A Life of Thornton Wilder*, (New Haven and New York: Ticknor & Fields, 1983): pp. 201-204.

DAVID CASTRONOVO ON CONTEMPORARY OBSTACLES TO APPRECIATING *OUR TOWN*

[David Castronovo is a literary critic and biographer who refers to himself as an "intellectual historian." He is editing the uncollected letters of Edmund Wilson and working on a study of American writers of the fifties. In this extract Castronovo, after reviewing the reviews of *Our Town*, reflects on the cultural conditions that produced so many of the early reviews to be mixed and notes that these conditions have been aggravated by more recent changes.]

The barriers that stand between us and *Our Town* are even more formidable than those of 1938. McCarthy of course was writing as a literary modern in sympathy with the anti-Stalinist left: the commitment to experiment of the *Partisan Review* might have drawn her toward the lyric innovation of Wilder's work, but behind her reaction was an uneasiness with Wilder's sentimental situations. Other progressives of 1938, perhaps even Mrs. Roosevelt, were struck by Wilder's essentially tragic view of human potential: despite what we aspire to, we are always unaware of life around us and of the value of our most simple moments. We must face death in order to see. Such an informing theme could only cause the liberal, progressive mind to recoil. After more than forty years, audiences have accumulated attitudes, convictions, tastes, and experiences that set them farther apart than ever. Distrust of WASP America's values, the sexual revolution, feminism, fear of America's complacency, the resistance of many Americans to marriage and family life, the distrust of group mentalities, the rise of ethnic literatures, the general loosening of restraints on language and conduct: such obstacles have wedged their way between us and Wilder's drama. As a scene unfolds—for example, Mrs. Gibbs being gently chastised by her husband for staying out so late at choir practice—the way we live now occupies the stage beside the players, mocking them and pointing up their limitations as fully developed men and women in the modern world.

Many of the roads that lead us to the drama of mid-century seem to be in better shape than the Wilder road: O'Neill and Williams deal with obsession, sexual passion, illness, and torment. Miller deals with broken American dreams. But Wilder employs the notations of an essentially stable and happy society. To reach his work, we must pay more attention to the situations and themes that he created for people such as ourselves: *Our Town* has our themes, our fears, our confusion; Wilder built the play so that every scene has something to reach us. Our problem has been that whereas other American playwrights have offered encounters with desolation and the tragic isolation of tormented people—the themes of the great modernists and indeed of Wilder himself in his first two novels—Wilder's 1938 play is about another area of our struggle: the essentially ordinary, uncomplicated, yet terrifying battle to realize fully our own ordinary existences. Such a subject obviously is more difficult to present than the more visceral situations that many great contemporary writers have dealt with; but Wilder's style and form are what force the concerns of the play to become familiar truths charged with new vision.

—David Castronovo, *Thornton Wilder*, (New York: The Ungar Publishing Company, 1986): pp. 84-85.

The Skin of Our Teeth

Interviewed for the January 12, 1953, issue of *Time* magazine, Wilder said, "*Our Town* is the life of the family seen from a telescope five miles away. *The Skin of Our Teeth* is the destiny of the whole human group seen from a telescope 1,000 miles away." From individual life in hometown America, Wilder turned to a transcultural context for the human family and its collective survival through the ages. He began working on the play in the years leading up to World War II but was engaged at the same time with numerous nonliterary activities relating to growing national and world anxieties. The plight of refugees fleeing Nazi Germany and Austria so moved him that he regularly met them on the docks in New York with money and arrangements for shelter. Wilder saw writing *The Skin of Our Teeth*, with its message that humanity is capable of survival despite repeated catastrophes, as a different kind of contribution to the world's morale. He finished Act III just at the time of the bombing of Pearl Harbor.

Wilder's journals record his struggle with each act, alternately worrying that the play was too innovative, crazy, or simplistic to carry the most serious theme he had ever addressed. In a later interview with Arthur Gelb, published in the *New York Times* on November 6, 1961, Wilder reflected on his choice of dramatic style: "Because we live in the twentieth century overrun by real anxiety, we have to use the comic spirit. No statement of gravity can be adequate to the gravity of the age in which we live." True to that spirit, the play is full of spectacular and amusing stagecraft. Wilder thought that realistic scenery and the traditional box set worked against a play's vitality because they permitted the audience to distance itself from the action by suggesting a time and place in the past. In *The Skin of Our Teeth* Wilder's presentational methods— ambitiously mixing features of burlesque and vaudeville with utterances of ancient wisdom—drew in the audience: pieces of the set fly around and disappear; mammoths and dinosaurs have speaking parts; muses take over microphones; hours talk; and actors fall ill or refuse to act out their scenes. Early reviews praised Wilder for enlivening both the American stage and the human race. Appreciating the comic effects, a critic for *Time* magazine of November 30, 1942, likened the play to a "philosophy class in a monkey house." Wilder's friend Alexander Woollcott commented in his *Letters* (1944) that Wilder's comic spirit seemed like a mix of pedagogue and poltergeist! And Edmund Wilson in *Shores of Light* (1952) called the play a combination of Plato and Groucho Marx. *The Skin of Our Teeth* won the Pulitzer Prize for 1943.

Act I dramatizes the destructiveness of the Ice Age as it affects the Antrobus (from the Greek word "anthropos" meaning "all mankind") family living in Excelsior (Latin for "ever upward"), New Jersey. The family is alarmed because Mr. Antrobus has not arrived home for dinner, but the far greater alarm is the menacing drop in temperature in the month of August as a wall of ice moves south from northern New England heading for Excelsior. The audience is told that people in Hartford, Connecticut have started to burn their pianos to keep warm. Sabina the maid directly offers to the audience her view of each family member while indirectly revealing that she is less than useful to them. Preoccupied with threatening to leave her position for one in a richer family and fretting over Mr. Antrobus, toward whom she feels amorous impulses, Sabina forgets or fails to keep the home fire going, arousing the ire of Mrs. Antrobus. At one point she startles the audience by announcing that "the author hasn't made up his silly mind as to whether we're all living back in caves or in New Jersey today." The point for Wilder is that both are possible on stage at the same time—the "eternal present" he coveted for dramatic effect that works to implicate audience members in the action rather than merely entertain them.

When Mr. Antrobus finally does arrive, he establishes himself as the bearer of the will to survive, urging all to keep warm. Animals are affected by the cold as well and try to come indoors. Mrs. Antrobus asks them if they've ever heard "from [their] grandmothers or anyone" about such cold weather, but they have no advice or solutions. Mr. Antrobus shares his family home with the frozen refugees and takes in the animals as well. He is willing to burn the house down to keep everyone warm—a proposal at once both idiotic and heroic—but he will not burn his books, for in them are the ancient and eternally useful words of wisdom humanity needs to survive. Mrs. Antrobus is more concerned with the survival of her own family, hovering with fierce maternal protectiveness over her not very likeable children. Sabina has already told the audience that if they want to understand the mother of this household they should "just go and look at a tigress, and look hard."

Into this desperate situation—with the very survival of humanity in question—suddenly arrive Homer and Moses. They offer, in Greek and Hebrew, their respective languages, the ancient mysteries of human resolve and meaning which no one in the audience is expected to understand. But this is another of Wilder's points: knowledge exists eternally, and each human being will recognize it at a level deeper than—and more effective than—the rational. Hearing ancient wisdom spoken in one's own language does not make it more likely that the accumulating mysteries of human existence will be understood. Efforts to keep the fires alive conclude the act, with ushers and members of the audience being asked to donate their own chairs for the common good.

Act II opens at the Atlantic City Boardwalk with the six hundred thousandth convention of the Honorable Order of Mammals, Subdivision Humans. Mr. Antrobus, now twenty thousand years old, begins his presidential welcoming speech by thanking his parents for having instructed him "to stand on [his] own two feet." The Ice Age has been surmounted and except for the common cold, earthquakes, plagues, interpersonal strife, and a few extinctions of the less adaptable species, the human race has survived and is headed toward a bright future. The slogan for survival has been "Work!" President Antrobus now adds "Enjoy Yourselves!" and Mrs. Antrobus reminds everyone to "Save the Family!" These imperatives—Work! Enjoy! Save! are reminiscent of the early Biblical commandments in Genesis.

Menacing signs of trouble intrude quickly. The Fortune Teller, intuiting the future from tiny hints of disturbance she sees within the conveners around her, announces the coming of rain and floods. The less astute conveners jeer at her calling her "Madam Kill-joy" and "Mrs. Jeremiah." Henry, slingshot in hand, appears suddenly in a burst of apparently gratuitous hostility toward a black workman pushing a Boardwalk chair. He is just barely restrained from murderous violence by his mother, who subsequently elicits from him his acquisitive motives which reveal Henry's complete unfamiliarity with any notions of right, wrong, and fair play. Mrs. Antrobus then correctly intuits "a rainy day ahead" just as she witnesses a transformation of her husband from proud and protective family man to a self-absorbed pleasure-seeker. Sabina, now a vacuous, prize-winning American beauty queen and explicit floozy in her "flounced red silk bathing suit," arrives on stage with her seductive intentions toward Mr. Antrobus intact. The earlier admonition to "Enjoy Yourselves" competes now with "Save the Family" and Mr. Antrobus succumbs to Sabina's seduction. Self-centeredness and its related vices—acquisitiveness and sexual indulgence—have set in motion once again the dark energies that threaten human stability and survival. The weather signals warn of a coming storm.

Sabina's seductive logic moves her from disruptiveness to outright malice of a kind with chilling relevance to an audience in 1942. She tells Mr. Antrobus (whom she now calls "George") not to worry about hurting the feelings of his wife because "*other* people haven't got feelings. Not in the same way that we have, we . . . presidents . . . and prize-winners . . . ." She calls others "just people of straw . . . [with] no insides at all" who don't belong in the "secret society at the top of the world" with herself and Antrobus. "The world," she says "was made for us . . . for [our] pleasure and power . . . ."

Human thinking of this kind deserves to perish but doesn't. One reason is that it's not the only thing happening on the stage. Mrs. Antrobus makes to Mr. Antrobus and everyone on stage and in the audience a remarkably wise, realistic, generous and forgiving speech about marriage:

> I didn't marry you because you were perfect. I didn't even marry you because I loved you. I married you because you gave me a promise. That promise made up for your faults. And the promise I gave you made up for mine. Two imperfect people got married and it was the promise that made the marriage . . . .And when our children were growing up, it wasn't a house that protected them—it was that promise.

These words disarm Antrobus and he turns away from Sabina who in this scene has successfully set a different kind of fire that just barely avoids destroying the family. Thus summoned to his noble and stabilizing role in the human family, he takes on the task of Noah to save a few sufficiently righteous people and two of each animal from destruction in the coming storm and the great Biblical Flood.

The other event is Sabina's startling announcement (as she steps out of character to become the actress Miss Somerset) that she will not actually play the seduction scene on stage because she doesn't want to cause pain to an actual friend in the audience currently in the painful throes of her husband's adultery. In addition to being a fine example of Wilder's dramatic devices to bring recognition to the audience and engage their active sympathy, these separate gestures of goodwill are sufficient to save the human race. The act concludes with the bingo-players—like Nero fiddling while his kingdom dies by fire—obliviously calling out their numbers as the human race dies by water. The Antrobus family miraculously makes it onto a boat with all the animals including a kangaroo carrying two turtles in its pouch—all just barely saved by the skin of their teeth.

Both the Flood and a World War have passed at the opening of Act III, and the human race, once again surviving catastrophe, must face the task of rebuilding. Everything lies in ruins and even the tomato is under suspicion for causing food poisoning in the actors. Nothing is reliable or secure. Some of the stricken actors are hospitalized "in perfect agony" and must be replaced by poor imitators—the unprepared stage hands who reluctantly but valiantly take over. These amusing stage maneuvers are also emblematic of human survival mechanisms: Pitch In! Co-operate! Get Over Yourself! Make Do With What You Have!

Mrs. Antrobus and Gladys emerge but are uncertain if any of the others have survived. Despite all her reasons to dislike Sabina, Mrs. Antrobus is genuinely pleased to discover she has survived: another saving gesture of forgiveness on her part. Signs of normality appear and are welcomed. Milk delivery is promised once the milkman catches a cow that survived. The shoe-polish factory blows its whistle. People will begin caring about their appearances again. Sabina wants to go to a movie that makes little sense but reminds the audience of the survival benefits of an occasional escape into fantasy and entertainment. Gladys has contributed to human survival by having given birth during the war.

Signs of the difficulty ahead appear with the arrival of Henry and Mr. Antrobus. Henry has become frozen with fierce self-isolation and hostility. The human race has now survived the calamity of war brought on by internal strife and interpersonal rivalries, but Henry reminds the audience of the continuing menace of predatory acquisitiveness and violence among people and nations. Mr. Antrobus has lost the "most important thing of all: the desire to begin again and start building." The sight of a very slight gesture of selflessness on Sabina's part reinvigorates him and he summons the human race to start all over again. He admonishes Henry for confusing liberty with selfishness and the fury of their father/son interaction threatens to bring the world back to the point of collapse. With the help of the Hours who speak the wisdom of Spinoza, Plato, Aristotle, and the Book of Genesis, Mr. Antrobus is inspired to make another effort. Their collective message seems to be that despite all the defeats and chaos to be endured by the living it is worth it to *just keep going*! Henry and Mr. Antrobus step out of character and try to understand each other and it appears that humanity will once again survive.

Wilder's brother Amos was a minister, but Wilder was never one to sermonize; in fact, he explicitly disapproved of what he called "paternalistic teaching." But he was deeply concerned with the ongoing precariousness of human existence and intrigued by speculations about what actually makes for a collective "will to survive." He was charged with having "too much optimism," but intimations of new and recurring cycles of violence and death are rarely upstaged in his plays by gestures of human cooperation or signs of an heroic capacity to endure, however remarkable and welcome these are. The skin of teeth (whatever that is) is not very much to rely on. In his journals Wilder called the Antrobuses "a fine American family who came through every conceivable calamity with screaming absurdity and a few shreds of dignity." The important point Wilder makes is that all the characters—even the least deserving and downright unlikable—are necessary for the survival of the whole human family.

The Skin of Our Teeth

Mr. Antrobus (George) plays—simultaneously and alternately—roles suggestive of Adam, Noah, cave man, inquisitive man, seducible man, inventor, ambitious suburban businessman, protective father and husband, and, in Act III, a version of himself as an actor. As a 20,000-year-old man, Mr. Antrobus represents archetypal experiences, achievements, and the character of the male human being. At one point he is president of the Order of Mammals, Subdivision Humans. He is proud of having invented the wheel. During the various catastrophes in the play that threaten human survival, he is especially attentive to saving all human knowledge and philosophy collected and recorded in books, and, following the war in Act III, is thrilled to discover they have survived.

Mrs. Antrobus (Maggie), also 20,000 years old, has qualities of Eve, Noah's wife, suburban housewife, spurned wife, and a fiercely protective mother tiger. Humanity owes to Maggie the domestic survival of the family, the invention of the apron, and the pleasures of eating tomatoes (she discovered their edibleness), but not the survival of learning since she would choose to burn all books including Shakespeare to keep her family from freezing to death or even getting a single head cold. It is she who will always keep the home fires burning. Mrs. Antrobus saves the collective knowledge of all women by putting it in a bottle which she throws into the sea, but she never tells the audience what that knowledge is.

Gladys and **Henry** are the Antrobus offspring. Sabina calls Henry "a real, clean-cut American boy" but hints that he is not very bright and lets slip the disturbing fact that he has killed a brother with a stone. Later, the audience sees him in a hostile frenzy against everyone. Henry is also the murderous and envious Biblical Cain who insists that he belongs with no one, but in Act III he reveals a normal human frailty. Gladys is either an exhibitionist or lacks social appropriateness about how to wear her dresses; she frequently misbehaves and paints red on her face. Giving birth to a child, Gladys represents the unthinking force of life to produce ongoing generations. Neither of the Antrobus children is particularly likeable and Henry is actually wicked, but they are sufficient explanation and motive for their parents to want to keep the universe alive and perpetually in motion.

Lily Sabina is the maid in the Antrobus household perennially giving two weeks notice and then changing her mind. Full of alarm and intrigue and most of the family secrets she represents a parody of the self-important Victorian maid. She also has qualities suggestive of Lilith, the eternal seductress, and she cannot be relied upon to keep the home fires burning. Her ambitions are less noble than those of Mrs. Antrobus and she is satisfied with less from life as well, being happy with ice cream and a new hat, and, after the devastation of the war, eager to get one of the hand-painted soup tureens being given away. Her speeches convey anti-intellectualism, conventional thinking, and self-centeredness, but her lively and comic spirit and brief revelations of her own vulnerability keep her a likeable character. Sabina occasionally functions as stage manager providing information to the audience and directing stage traffic when the play goes especially awry.

The **Fortune Teller** not surprisingly believes one can know the future, but insists, cryptically, that knowing the past is not possible. She is giving voice to Wilder's anti-realism belief that the truth of the past was only knowable by and for each person at the time of knowing.

The Skin of Our Teeth

JOHN GASSNER ON THEATRICALITY

[John Gassner was born in Hungary and became a major promoter of American theatre. He served as jury member for drama on the Pulitzer Prize Committee. Here he discusses features of "theatricalism" in Wilder's play *The Skin of Our Teeth*.]

The fundamental premise of realism is the Aristotelian one that drama is an imitation of an action; realists held, therefore, that the most desirable theatre is that in which imitation is the closest. The fundamental premise of theatricalism is that theatre is not imitation in the narrow sense, which Aristotle himself never could have held, since the Greek drama upon which he based conclusions in his *Poetics* was not realistically imitative.[5] For the theatricalist, the object of action and of all other "imitative" elements is not imitation but *creativeness*, and a special kind of creativeness at that. The realists would agree, of course, as to the value of creativeness. But the theatricalist goes one step further, and that step is the truly decisive one for the theory and practice of pure theatricalism. He maintains that there is never any sense in pretending that one is not in the theatre; that no amount of make-believe is reality itself; that in short, theatre is the medium of dramatic art, and effectiveness in art consists in using the medium rather than concealing it. In the theatricalist view, concealment of the medium is tantamount to the nullification of art. Therefore, the theatricalist feels that plays should be written and staged in such a manner that there will be no pretense that what is happening on the stage is real. The object of writing and performing for the medium is to create theatre—theatrical actions, characterizations, and images—and nothing else. The object of going to a "show" is nothing else than seeing or experiencing a show, not reality. (. . .)

Even in so distinguished a play as *The Skin of Our Teeth* the intrusion of self-conscious theatricality somewhat blunts the edge of comedy and causes the essential action to mark time. Now and then the play's "playfulness" becomes altogether too arch. But one can go further in criticizing Wilder's theatricality and maintain that the intrusion of "theatre" weakens the power of the play, especially in the last act, which occurs immediately after a world-devastating war. If the human race has survived only by the skin of its teeth, one is tempted to ask, what is the author so cheerful about? In the first and second acts, the audience could be reminded that man has been the same throughout history in his aspirations and contradictions. The humor attendant upon the theatrical blending of life in suburban New Jersey with life during the Ice Age, or the linking of the legend of Noah with an Atlantic City convention, was in accord with the author's comment on the human race. But in the third act, which deals with contemporary disaster, the theatricalism is not only inappropriate because it is played in the wrong key and is perhaps insufficiently climactic for a dramatic masterpiece, but it is evasive as well. The author has apparently nothing to say that he hasn't already told us twice. So he repeats himself again, quotes the right authors, who give us the right schoolbook assurances in a pageant-like procession of the show's backstage personnel; and he reminds us for the third time that *The Skin of Our Teeth* is just a show. (. . .)

Nevertheless, *The Skin of Our Teeth* is perhaps the best out-and-out theatricalist work of the American theater.[6]

NOTES

5. S. H. Butcher, in Aristotle's Theory of Poetry and Fine Art (4th ed., Dover Publications, 1951), argues well that "imitation" is a creative act: "It is the expression of the concrete thing under an image which answers to its true idea." To reproduce the universal "in a simple and sensuous form is not to reflect a reality already familiar through sense perceptions" (p. 154). It is "rivalry of nature." Certainly esthetic semblance could not have meant slavish imitation for Aristotle, who wrote that the author "ought to prefer probable impossibilities to possible improbabilities" (p. 128). Nevertheless, Aristotle was apparently inclined to place reliance on "imitation" somewhat in our ordinary sense of the term. Art, for Aristotle, involves sensuous perception rather than symbolization. "A work of art," Butcher declares (p. 124), "is a likeness and not a symbolic representation of it." Symbolists and other antirealists, then, could draw even less comfort from Aristotle than literal realists.

6. Except for Cummings' too esoteric, dadaist-surrealist play *him*, which for all its muddle has a quality of imagination and power of expression absent in many better-built plays.

—John Gassner, *Form and Idea in Modern Theatre*, (New York: The Dryden Press, 1956): pp. 141-143.

Mary McCarthy on Convention and Nostalgia

[Mary McCarthy, prominent American intellectual, expresses disappointment with what she perceives to be conventional views in *Skin of Our Teeth*.]

The plot and structure of *The Skin of Our Teeth* must by this time be in the public domain. Everybody knows that the play deals with three great crises in human history, the return of the Ice Age, the Flood, the War, any war at all or this war in particular. It is Mr. Wilder's fancy that all these events happened to a man named George Antrobus of 216 Cedar Street, Excelsior, New Jersey, father of two, President of the Ancient Order of Mammals, inventor, soldier and occasional philanderer. Man, then, enlightened ape, is seen as the eternal husband, whose destiny is an endless commuter's trip between the Home and the Office, the poles of the human sphere. The trip may not be broken on pain of flood, ice, fascism; a stopover with the Other Woman will result in a disaster of millennial proportions. "Oh, oh, oh! Six o'clock and the master not home yet," says the maid, opening the play. In other words, if George misses the five-fifteen, Chaos is come again. This is the moral of the piece. Man, says Mr. Wilder, from time to time gets puffed up with pride and prosperity, he grows envious, covetous, lecherous, forgets his conjugal duties, goes whoring after women; portents of disaster appear, but he is too blind to see them; in the end, with the help of the little woman, who has never taken any stock in either pleasure or wisdom, he escapes by the skin of his teeth. *Sicut erat in principio* . . . .

It is a curious view of life. It displays elements of Christian morality. Christ, however, was never so simple, but on the contrary allowed always for paradox (the woman taken in adultery, the story of Martha and Mary, "Consider the lilies of the field") and indeed regarded the family as an obstacle to salvation. (. . .)

And here we find again Mr. Wilder's perennial nostalgia, not for the past but for an eternal childhood, for the bedrock of middle-class family life, for "*the old Sunday evenings at home with the tinkling piano our guide.*" It is a nostalgia which found a pure and lyrical expression in *Our Town*, but which has made its way more furtively into *The Skin of Our Teeth* and lurks there as an impediment both to action and to thought, for at the end of each act the play hits the suburban family group, stumbles over it, and comes to a halt; the repetition is inevitable, but not dramatic: the only conflict is the conflict between the submerged idea and the form. The play in general suffers from a certain embarrassment and uneasiness, as if its author were ashamed of the seriousness with which he adheres to his theme.

—Mary McCarthy, *Sights and Spectacles*, (New York: Farrar, Straus and Cudahy, 1943): pp. 54-55.

LOUIS BROUSSARD ON OPTIMISM

[Louis Broussard is Professor of English and Drama at St. John's University. In addition to his work on American plays he published a book on Edgar Allen Poe, *The Measure of Poe* (1969). Wilder stood out in his time for sustaining optimism about America and human nature. In this extract, Broussard discusses evidence of optimism in *The Skin of Our Teeth*.]

LIKE Eliot, Thornton Wilder was already an established writer when he turned to the stage. Like Eliot, Wilder adapted to a dramatic form ideas which he had already given literary expression. Four novels and several one-act plays early testified to the same influence which has been so important in the work of Eliot, the Bergsonian concept of time in movement. There the two writers leave each other as Wilder seeks to universalize his attitude in terms representative of any place and time rather than to individualize it in terms specifically applicable to this age, and in a manner so optimistic as to establish himself unique among contemporary American playwrights. No other writer begins with so hopeful a premise: that this age is essentially no different from any other, that its problems, whatever they may be, since Wilder refuses to give expression to them, will resolve themselves in change which can only be better than the past. His is not the search for an exit from dilemma; there is no dilemma. If he has any advice to give, it is that people continue to love one another, and here occurs another striking difference between him and Eliot. Divine love, argues Eliot, assures the best security both in this life and for the next. To Wilder the love between people is at least equally important. (. . .)

Always concerned with man and his relationship to all time and all place, Wilder proceeds from a localized inquiry into the life cycle—the birth-reproduction-death theme of *Our Town*—to an inclusive presentation of civilization in *The Skin of Our Teeth*. He proposes to tell, not the life story of an individual, but the story of civilization, and to highlight the catastrophes of glacier, flood, and war, but without the death-finale which gives the close to individual man's story. Death yields to the death-resurrection theme expressed in the perpetual life cycle of progressive civilization. (. . .)

Wilder again drew upon nostalgic detail for content in *The Skin of Our Teeth*, suburban this time if not rural, but for the sentiment of *Our Town* he substituted buffoonery. Time in movement in *Our Town* receives expression from contemplative commentaries like this one by the stage manager: "Three years have gone by. Yes, the sun's come up over a thousand times. . . ." The same idea begins *The Skin of Our Teeth*, but in a humorous attitude, as the following news event is flashed upon a screen: "The sun rose this morning at 6:32 a.m. . . . The Society of Affirming the End of the World at once went into a special session and postponed the arrival of that event for twenty-four hours. . . ." Purportedly a comic treatment of a serious theme, the formula rarely permits a scene that is not flippant; and when the action threatens to produce one, Sabina steps out of role and declares to the Stage Manager her refusal to play anything tragic or disturbing. Somehow, amid the clownish antics and the jokes, a philosophy works itself out, a doctrine of survival which proclaims that, whatever the conflict, the obstacle, be it one of nature's or one man-made, man will survive, armed as he is with ideas inherited from his race and the creative energy inherited from his Maker. The persistence of truth despite man's inability to realize it, and the repeated recovery from chaos, which always yields to progress realized through a creative energy which man inherits from a Creator or life force—this is the wisdom with which Antrobus sets out to rebuild the world in greater progress.

That Wilder should regard the problems of our age as insignificant within the scope of all time and space labels him a unique optimist among the writers of this century. In such company as O'Neill, Eliot, Anouilh, and many other post-war pessimists, Wilder emerges as a lone dissenter. Not because he is an optimist—Eliot can be considered an optimist and so can Faulkner and Hemingway—but because his optimism grows out of an indifference to his own period. All other writers, outside of drama as well, assume the attitude that the ideals of the past rest upon beliefs to which the world becomes increasingly apathetic. O'Neill, when he discovered the world to be without God, struggled to find a substitute, and when he failed, endeavored to return, but, finding that impossible, gave in to despair. Lawrence and Eliot, dissatisfied with the materialism of their period, found a return plausible, one to paganism, the other to medieval Christianity. Faulkner and Hemingway subscribe to life with honor, but they have not been unaware of man's deficiency or his insecurity in this age. All who have struggled with the twentieth century dilemma, characterized by doubt, conflict, and fear have had to take into account the Second Coming of Yeats. Its failure thus far to appear has been the cause of many a defeat and many a compromise. Wilder, who once wrote that action in the theater "takes place in a perpetual present time,"[11] selects those things which have survived from the past and presumes they will survive the challenge of this age as well.

NOTE

11. Thornton Wilder, "Some thoughts on Playwriting," *Intent of the Artist* (ed. A Centano), 96.

—Louis Broussard, *American Drama: Contemporary Allegory from Eugene O'Neill to Tennessee Williams*, (Norman, Oklahoma: University of Oklahoma Press, 1962): pp. 92-93, 99, 101-103.

[Glenway Wescott left his Wisconsin farm to attend the University of Chicago, but left before graduating. He was known for his public support of author's rights and was president of the National Institute of Arts and Letters from 1958-61. In this extract he comments on Wilder's success at acting in his own plays and describes his performance of Mr. Antrobus.]

The Skin of Our Teeth . . . was his contribution to our morale and our vision of the future during World War II. If I remember rightly he did not undertake the role himself until four or five years later. Of course world history had scarcely gone beyond it or superseded it; still has not. He played it with no effect of author's afflatus; on the other hand, with none of the vanity or the cajolery of the amateur actor. Even in passages of serious reference to the destructiveness then going forward in the world and to other ever-possible future holocausts, he was able to characterize his Antrobus with humor, temperamentally: a familiar type of tired but sturdy, more or less indomitable man in a raincoat or a trench coat, universal male raiment of our particular time of troubles. As he came on stage he immediately established the reality of the scene by glancing all around it, taking possession of it, flashing his eyes; then turned and faced the audience and immediately began his portrayal of himself, gesturing strongly, as though wielding a brush, painting great everyman's portrait on the canvas of air between him and the audience, up over our heads. (. . .)

It was curiously self-assured, with a soft and rapturous tone in certain passages; and the mimicry in it was broader and simpler than that of the present-day psychological school of acting. Never for a moment did he seem self-concerned, although one couldn't help thinking of his Antrobus as autobiographical.

It made the oddest evening's entertainment. Most plays in which the human race is personified in any way are weak in performance, though with virtuoso techniques and the best will in the world. Everyman as a rule turns out to be just anyone, and the audience couldn't care less. Wilder prevented this by the intensities that I have just mentioned, by humorous simplifications of his movements and facial expressions, and by his absorption and self-absorption, which is the opposite of self-concern. At every point he was able to infuse the simple text with strange temperament; it was his own temperament. (. . .)

Throughout his performance he kept contrasting the explicit and the implicit, as though for every scene, every speech, he had decided in advance what part of the meaning and the emotion he could best express, and let everything inexpressible in it go. And one felt that it was just this simple aspect of the play that he had rehearsed, practiced, perfected, so that he could have rendered it in his sleep, if asked to. But then, wide awake, when the curtain went up, he apparently concentrated all of his intelligence and spirit on those things that he could not exactly express. (. . .)

Clear as a bell, but with a haunted clarity; plain as day, but casting a shadow! In that emphatic voice, with its little barking tones now and then, earnestly projecting the lines, some humorous, some sententious, some oracular, there was an intensely urgent utopian spirit, almost a wild spirit, expressive of that desirousness which above all else characterizes the human race, which stops at nothing and which never ends; that anarchy inherent in our nature which necessitates our will power; that strange habit of forgiving or at least forgetting, which causes us to pull our punches to some extent every blessed time, for better or worse, preventing the entire victory of any one aspect of our humanity over any other aspect, even of good over evil, or evil over good. (. . .)

[T]he manner of his acting bears a relation to the predominant, prevailing quality of his prose style, in dramatic prose and narrative prose alike, polished and purposeful but also somewhat plain and modest; not presuming to tell everything or to give proof of anything incontrovertibly; not particularly aiming at anything unknowable or occult, but never disavowing or turning away from things irrepressible and unruly, things chaotic, even things inchoate.

—Glenway Wescott, *Images of Truth: Remembrances and Criticism*, (New York and Evanston: Harper & Row, Publishers, 1962): pp. 305-307.

[Malcolm Goldstein, a writer on American drama, discusses
the potential for confusion caused by the mix of theatrical
devices Wilder makes use of in his play.]

Much the most complex of Wilder's plays, *The Skin of Our Teeth*
presented a distinct risk on Broadway despite its merit. The play
rests not only upon Joyce, but upon German expressionism,
vaudeville, burlesque, and Wilder's own one-acts—a combination of
forces transfusing both structure and theme. It also nods at the smug
domestic dramas of the late nineteenth and early twentieth centuries
and mocks their limited vision as controlled by the box set. As a
wartime play written, Wilder has since, said, "under strong
emotion,"[21] it was calculated to encourage the troubled public of
1942, but its theme is broad enough to transcend the concerns of the
time and to appeal to the relatively small audience for serious plays
in any year. (. . .)

As he had done with *Our Town*, Wilder designed a presentational
method which would permit the audience to be drawn toward the
characters as individuals with private problems while recognizing
that they also function in a broader sphere as the representatives of
the entire race. This, however, is only part of a quite elaborate
scheme. There is a deliberately old-fashioned, expressionistic
vaudeville quality in much of the action. (. . .)

It is this vaudevillesque aspect of *The Skin of Our Teeth* which led
many reviewers to assert that Wilder had written his play under the
influence of Ole Olsen and Chick Johnson's *Hellzapoppin*, a long-
running extravaganza contrived from bits of burlesque and revue
material, when in fact he had drawn nothing from it at all.[22] On the
other hand, George and Maggie Antrobus and their servant Sabina
occasionally take part in low-comedy clowning of the vaudeville and
Keystone Cops variety at the same time that they represent Adam,
Eve, and Lillith and, as the name Antrobus indicates, All Mankind.
Yet, because they stand for the entire race, they must have genuine
human qualities as well. To stress the essentially human, Wilder

frequently lets them drop their stage roles and appear as actors who have been engaged to appear in a play titled *The Skin of Our Teeth*. The development of characters on so many planes at once requires skill in balancing and adjusting dialogue in such a way as to avoid awkwardness in the transition from one level of personality to another. Present always is the danger of baffling the audience where the intention is to instruct. Wilder's success is evident in the intensity of feeling generated by the characters, which at the appropriate moments reaches the heights of *Our Town* without jarring against the comic elements. In observing that the audience sees double while watching the action,[23] Wilder underestimated his achievement; the keenest members of the audience will see not merely two sorts of personality in each character, but three, four, or even five as the play unfolds.

NOTES

21. Wilder, *Three Plays*, p. xiii.
22. Isabel Wilder.
23. Wilder, *Three Plays*, p. xiii.

—Malcolm Goldstein, *The Art of Thornton Wilder*, (Lincoln, Nebraska: University of Nebraska Press, 1965): pp. 118-120.

DONALD HABERMAN ON THE POWER OF THEATRICALITY

[Donald Haberman has written two books on Thornton Wilder. Here he discusses the essential connection between Wilder's controversial use of "theatricality" and the successful enactment of his theme.]

The imaginative presentation of human behavior patterns as in a dream Wilder employed most forcefully at the conclusion of Act II of *The Skin of Our Teeth*. The scene is Atlantic City. The characters in this act come closest to being like the characters in a comic strip. They are larger than life, and they have a naïve mythic quality. After Antrobus has succumbed to Sabina, after Mrs. Antrobus has tossed into the sea her letter in which are written "all the things that a woman knows," after Gladys is exposed in red stockings, and after it is revealed that Henry his again hit a man with a stone, the almost-but-not-quite-real Atlantic City dissolves. Lights begin to flash and whirl unpleasantly. A "high whistling noise begins." All the animals are described as appearing in pairs. Loud thunder is heard. Antrobus tries in vain to speak to the radio audience. The conveners snake-dance across the stage while a voice from the bingo parlor calls the numbers and letters of the game and Esmeralda frighteningly pronounces doom to them all. Throughout, Mrs. Antrobus calls Henry-Cain.

In this mad scene Wilder deserts recognizable reality first of all because such a removal from what is familiar dramatizes best the collapse of the Antrobus world. A realistic scene of destruction could only appear rather mild and perhaps even silly. Secondly, the nightmare on stage, from which the Antrobus family escapes by fleeing through the aisles of the theater, is a representation of the disintegration of man's moral and emotional world. This inner world is mysterious and cannot satisfactorily be represented according to traditional Aristotelian logic. It demands the arbitrary logic of the imagination. The flying scenery, suggested, according to Wilder, by the performances of Olsen and Johnson's *Hellzapoppin'*, is more than comic stage business. The shakiness of the world on stage suggests, even beyond the impermanence of the theatrical representation, the more sinister idea of the impermanence of the particular details of life. Beginning with the fall of Antrobus, or Adam, everything that depended on their faith, the static stability of Eden, is removed and must be recreated.

—Donald Haberman, *The Plays of Thornton Wilder*, (Middletown, Connecticut: Wesleyan University Press, 1967): pp. 70-71.

M.C. Kuner on the Problem of Evil

[M.C. Kuner, a playwright and teacher of drama, discusses inconsistencies in Wilder's portrayal of evil in *The Skin of Our Teeth*.]

The Skin of Our Teeth carries the author's primary message that humanity can, must, and will triumph over adversity. But in this play Wilder also goes one step further in his explorations and examines in greater detail than usual the nature of evil itself. From where did it come? And why? The second question has already been answered for us, if indirectly: Wilder seems to suggest that evil almost has to be present as an ingredient of life in order for mankind to conquer it. But the answer to the first question proves to be the weakest portion of the play.

Although *The Skin of Our Teeth* is both amusing and technically effective, although it divorces itself from the tired concept of drama as a series of confrontations between opposing forces [. . .] and is inventive about what is substituted, the play fails because it attempts to define the problem of evil in terms of the character of Henry. If he is Cain and the symbol of wickedness, who really created him: how did he—Evil—originate?

Mr. Antrobus seems to feel that Henry's wickedness stems from being misunderstood: there is no other explanation for the scene when Henry suddenly becomes an unhappy actor who was badly treated by his friends. We are told that Henry would be able to understand the alphabet, which his father invented, if it were a little simpler—but that, too, is a simplification. Moreover, it is not Henry's act but the coming of the Flood that is timed to accompany the sins of Mr. Antrobus: his wrongdoing consists of wishing to abandon his family—that is, his human responsibility—but his transgressions seem too petty for the deluge that will engulf everyone. And the Ice Age of the first act, for which no one is to blame, for no moral lapse has been witnessed—how is that explained?

—M.C. Kuner, *Thornton Wilder: The Bright and the Dark*, (New York: Thomas Y. Crowell Company, 1972): pp. 158-159.

LINDA SIMON ON CRITICAL REACTION TO
THE SKIN OF OUR TEETH

[Linda Simon, biographer and teacher, reviews a selection of reviews of *The Skin of Our Teeth*.]

The Skin of Our Teeth opened at the Plymouth Theatre in New York on November 18, 1942. It was, thought Lewis Nichols of the Times, "the best pure theatre" of the forties. Thornton's story "of man's constant struggle for survival, and his wonderment over why he so struggles, is presented with pathos and broad comedy, with gentle irony and sometimes a sly self-raillery." Wolcott Gibbs of *The New Yorker* agreed that the play was "by far the most interesting and exciting . . . I've seen this year . . . . Fredric March and Florence Eldridge, as Mr. and Mrs. Antrobus, achieve just the proper combination of the normal and the supernatural; they speak with the unmistakable accents of suburban America, but it is also easy to believe that they have been married for five thousand years."[23] *The Skin of Our Teeth*, thought *Time*'s reviewer, "is like a philosophy class conducted in a monkey house." The plot concerns the eternal survival of Every Family as represented by Mr. and Mrs. Antrobus, their son, Henry (né Cain), and daughter, Gladys. They are assisted in coping with their daily trials by their maid, Sabina, the archetypal seductress, whose exasperation with the play's lack of convention is sometimes conveyed directly to the audience. Walls lean, bits of scenery rise and fall, a long-suffering stage manager must convince Sabina to continue her role. . . . Some viewers wondered if the effects were not contrived by the director, Elia Kazan, whose nickname, "Gadge," came from his willingness to try any innovation. But it was Thornton who called for whatever details he wanted, drawing on the old stock companies be remembered from his childhood in California, vaudeville, musical comedies, plays he had seen in Germany in 1928, and his own lively imagination. "*The Skin of Our Teeth* is a cockeyed and impudent vaudeville littered with asides and swarming with premeditated anachronisms. Dinosaurs collide with bingo; the Muses jostle the microphone." Thornton had created "spectacular stagecraft" with a message that was always understood. "Perfectly clear . . . is Wilder's optimistic conclusion that mankind, for all its bad luck and narrow escapes, is indestructible."[24]

Indeed, it was the message, rather than the "highjinks" and "academic, if not collegiate" humor, that impressed Stark Young. ". . . The underlying theme, that of man's struggle and survival, climbing, falling, destroying himself, being destroyed, surviving by the skin of his teeth but passionately and stubbornly and touchingly alive, is a profound and ancient theme. From it arrive passages in the play that are moving and elevated. The conception of the Cain motif, rash figure of blood and destruction but kept yet in his human frailty, is a notable piece of imaginative creation, and to quote all those superb passages from great thinkers is certainly to invite the gods to supper."[25]

Thornton was especially gratified by Rosamond Gilder's review in *Theatre Arts*. "When the breath of creative imagination blows through the theatre, what exhilaration to the lungs, what refreshment to the spirit! Doors may bang and scenery fly about; audiences may be outraged, infuriated, delighted, but the theatre is once more alive. Thornton Wilder's *The Skin of Our Teeth* is not only a tribute to the indestructibility of the human race . . . ; it is also a giddy proof of the theatre's own imperishable vitality."[26] (. . .)

Alexander Woollcott called the play "a bulletin issued from the sickroom of a patient in whose health we are all pardonably interested, a bulletin signed by a physician named Thornton Wilder."[33]

NOTES

23. November 28, 1942, 35.
24. *Time*, November 30, 1942, 57.
25. *New Republic*, November 30, 1942, 714–15.
26. Gilder, 9.
33. Woollcott, 245.

—Linda Simon, *Thornton Wilder: His World*, (Garden City, New York: Doubleday & Company, 1979): pp.170-173.

GILBERT A. HARRISON ON THE CHARGE OF PLAGIARISM

[Gilbert A. Harrison, literary reviewer, discusses the charges against Wilder for alleged plagiarism of material from James Joyce's *Finnegan's Wake* made by Joseph Campbell and Henry Morton Robinson in the December 19, 1942 issue of the *Finnegans's Wake*.]

Edmund Wilson took the accusation more seriously but not as an indictment:

The general indebtedness to Joyce . . . is as plain as anything of the kind can be; it must have been conscious on Wilder's part. He has written and lectured on *Finnegans Wake*; he is evidently one of the persons who has most felt its fascination and most patiently explored its text. This derivation would not necessarily affect one way or another the merits of Wilder's play. Joyce is a great quarry, like Flaubert, out of which a variety of writers have been getting and will continue to get a variety of different things; and Wilder is a genuine poet with a form and imagination of his own who may find his themes where he pleases without incurring the charge of imitation.*

When the *Saturday Review* asked Thornton to comment on the Campbell-Robinson article, he prepared a temperate reply and filed it away. In that unpublished statement he explained that in deciphering Joyce's novel the idea had come to him that one aspect of it might be expressed in drama: the method of representing mankind's long journey by superimposing different epochs of time simultaneously. He had even made sketches employing Joyce's characters and locale but soon abandoned the project. The slight element of plot in Joyce's novel was so thinly glimpsed amid the distortions of nightmare and the polyglot distortions of language that any possibility of dramatization was "out of the question." The notion about mankind in *The Skin of Our Teeth* and the viewing of the Antrobus family through several simultaneous layers of time did persist, however, and began to surround itself with many inventions of his own. (. . .)

Farfetched as it was,** the allegation of plagiarism sufficiently intimidated the Critics Circle of New York that in April 1943 they denied *The Skin of Our Teeth* their annual award and gave it to Sidney Kingsley's *The Patriots*, a retelling of the Thomas Jefferson story. The vote had been close, six to six on the first ballot, but George Jean Nathan, always unfriendly to Thornton, carried the day. Some called the Critics Circle the League of Nathans. (. . .)

Not until thirteen years after the Campbell-Robinson article did Thornton reply to a query about "the circumstances under which you conceived the double time situation in *The Skin of Our Teeth*" by saying that "the treatment of several simultaneous levels of time was borrowed from Joyce's *Finnegans Wake* and Henry James' *A Sense of the Past* and is even in Mark Twain's *Connecticut Yankee at King Arthur's Court*. A year before his death, Thornton wrote [. . .] "the narrative mind is working in a field of apparently free association, there is really no such thing as free association. Every story is consciously based upon some story already in existence; it adds little increments or manipulates it—reverses the situation or puts plus signs for minus signs." Once, jokingly, Thornton suggested that every word of Hamlet's soliloquy beginning with "To be or not to be" was a direct translation from a mid-sixteenth-century Italian collection of philosophical essays known as *Consolazione*, which included a passage beginning "Essere o non essere. quest'e il problema." (. . .)

Far from apologizing [. . .] Thornton went out of his way to credit his sources. The third act of *Our Town*, he informed a correspondent, was based on a subject treated in *The Woman of Andros*; the closing first-act speech of *Our Town* could be found in Joyce's *Portrait of the Artist as a Young Man*; the catalogue of Emily's goodbyes was after that of Achilles in the underworld; the character of Mrs. Levi in *The Matchmaker* was borrowed from Molière's *The Miser*. "As the shoplifter said to a judge in Los Angeles: 'I only steal from the best department stores, and they don't miss it.'"

NOTES

* *Classics and Commercials* (New York: Farrar, Straus, 1950), p. 83.

** In *Thornton Wilder*, University of Minnesota Pamphlet on American Writers no. 341 (Minneapolis: University of Minnesota Press, 1964), Bernard Grebanier dismisses the charge: "It is as intelligent as accusing Sophocles of plagiarizing Aeschylus in his *Electra* and Euripedes of plagiarizing both in his; or Racine of Plagiarizing Euripedes in his *Phèdre*; or Shakespeare of plagiarizing North, Holinshed, Riche, Cinthio, Belleforest, Lodge, and many others. . . . Whatever Wilder's indebtedness to Joyce, what he may owe he had made his own, and his hand is evident everywhere in this great play—one of the greatest, I believe, in the history of the American theater" (pp. 33–34).

> —Gilbert A. Harrison, *The Enthusiast: A Life of Thornton Wilder*, (New Haven and New York: Ticknor & Fields, 1983): pp.230-231, 233-234.

DAVID CASTRONOVO ON COMPARISONS WITH BRECHT'S *MOTHER COURAGE*

[David Castronovo, literary critic, here discusses the similarity in devices and didactic purposes between Wilder and Bertolt Brecht's plays.]

The Skin of Our Teeth also becomes a more enjoyable and intelligible theatrical experience when it is placed beside Bertolt Brecht's epic-theater works. The staging, character presentation, themes, and generalizing power bear an important relationship to Brecht's experiments in the 1930s.[11] Without having to argue for direct influences, one still can see a great deal about Wilder's techniques and idea by placing them in apposition to a work like *Mother Courage*. Since both plays take place in time of war, employ epic exaggeration, explore violence and selfishness, and take an unadorned look at what suffering does to people, it is not unreasonable to view them together. *Mother Courage* was also written three years before *The Skin of Our Teeth*, a fact that is not without significance considering Wilder's close touch with the currents of twentieth-century literature. Yet whether he was influenced directly or not, the affinities are strong. As pieces of stagecraft, both plays employ a large historical sweep and present material in a nonrealistic manner; Brecht's play of the Thirty Years War and Wilder's play of civilization's disaster both reach for large generalizations about man's durability and defects. The works do this essentially didactic job by means of screen projections, announcers, jagged episodic plots, and characters who are often stereotypical or emblematic. Wilder's third act overcomes Brecht's relentless detachment from his characters, but even here—as we sympathize with Sabina and Henry—we are not in a theater where the individual psyche is the main concern. Wilder is more involved with the process of learning, the hope of progress, and the impediments in human nature and culture than with the individuality of his people. In this he is one with Brecht, a writer who studies the harshness of civilization and the brutality of ordinary folk. Sabina's selfish, compromising, essentially amoral view of the human struggle for survival is like nothing so much as Mother Courage's matter-of-fact attitude toward suffering and willingness to hitch up her wagon and do business after her children are dead. Wilder has humanized and intellectualized this savage world, but he essentially works with its terrifying ingredients. Even Antrobus, the beacon light of the three acts, is tainted by the lust, a cynicism, cheapness, and hypocrisy that Brecht saw as the central features of bourgeois life.

NOTE

11. See also Douglas Wixon, Jr., "The Dramatic Techniques of Thornton Wilder and Bertolt Brecht," *Modern Drama*, XV, no. 2 (September 1972), pp. 112–124. This informative essay gives special attention to the anti-illusionist theater of Brecht and Wilder; it argues that Wilder employed Brechtian techniques from 1931 onward. The article does not explore the thematic affinities of the two writers.

—David Castronovo, *Thornton Wilder*, (New York: The Ungar Publishing Company, 1986): pp. 104-105.

CHRISTOPHER J. WHEATLEY ON AUDIENCE RECOGNITION OF UNIVERSAL TRUTHS

[Christopher J. Wheatley teaches English and drama at Catholic University of America. He published *Secular Ethics in the Restoration* (1993) and is currently co-editing a collection of Irish plays. In this extract Wheatley examines the Platonic notion of the human capacity to recognize truth without understanding it.]

The Skin of Our Teeth enacts several examples of Wilder's belief that the audience need not "understand" what is being presented, but need only recognize the act of knowing. In the first act when Moses and Homer present their "knowledge," they speak in Hebrew and Greek respectively. There can be no question of most audiences understanding what is said. What is important is the placing of the achievements of the past in a situation where they have no practical use. Wilder regards these truths as having universal validity; if the scene is dramatically effective, then the audience will recognize this without needing to understand the specifics. Donald Haberman perceptively points out the process involved in the first act of *The Skin of Our Teeth*, a process that I think is operant in most of Wilder's nonrealist drama: "This primitive emotional reaction is emphasized by the passages in Greek and Hebrew. The foreign words recited dramatically, precisely because the audience do not understand their meaning, touch something in the audience that is deeper than rational argument could go."[12]

Presented with passages stripped of context and familiarity, the audience responds to wisdom (represented by Homer and Moses) as something that is recognized, rather than as something that is explained. Another example of this principle is the speeches of the hours at the end of the play. These speeches do have an intellectual context within the play that they help to explicate, but this is only clear when reading the play, because the speeches, drawn from Plato, Aristotle, and Spinoza, are too complex to be fully grasped upon one hearing, which is all one gets when one sees the play. Again, it is the insistence dramatically upon the author's and the audience's recognition of their validity outside of understanding that makes the speeches effective.

Francis Fergusson writes that "Brecht, Wilder, and Eliot do not expect the audiences to share their intimate perceptions, whether 'realistic' or 'poetic.'"[13] On the other hand, the realist author presupposes a knowledge and perception that can be communicated to the audience but is not present in the audience prior to the theatrical enactment. Williams, for instance, in the introduction to *Cat on a Hot Tin Roof*, says, "I want to go on talking to you as freely and intimately about what we live and die for as if I knew you better than anyone else you know."[14] Williams's subject is private and can only be conveyed personally: "I want you to observe what I do for your possible pleasure and to give you knowledge of things that I feel I may know better than you, because my world is different from yours, as different as every man's world is from the world of others" (p. vii). Each person's world is inherently different because of circumstance. There are some things, consequently, that Williams knows better than the rest of us—the South, homophobia—and he can explain his "lyrical" understanding to us. On the other hand, Sabina says in her first long speech, "I hate this play and every word in it. As for me, I don't understand a single word of it, anyway"

(p. 73). However, she later says, "Now that you audience are listening to this, I understand it a little better" (p. 76). Wilder's bare stage is not something he knows better than we do, because it is everyone's world; moreover, what he knows can only be understood communally. Fundamentally, Wilder thinks that each person's world shares important repetitions that an audience recognizes.

Notes

12. Donald Haberman, The Plays of Thornton Wilder (Middletown, Conn.: Wesleyan UP, 1967), p. 72.

13. Francis Fergusson, "Brecht, Wilder, and Eliot: Three Allegorists," Sewanee Review 64 (1956): 544.

14. Tennessee Williams, Cat on a Hot Tin Roof (New York: Signet, 1985), p. x.

—Christopher J. Wheatley, "Thornton Wilder, the Real, and Theatrical Realism," *Realism and the American Dramatic Tradition*, ed. William W. Demastes (Tuscaloosa and London: The University of Alabama Press, 1996): pp.145-147.

Thornton Wilder

The Trumpet Shall Sound, 1920.

The Cabala, 1926.

The Bridge of San Luis Rey, 1927.

The Woman of Andros, 1930.

The Long Christmas Dinner and Other Plays, 1931.

Lucrece, 1933.

Heaven's My Destination, 1935.

Our Town, 1938.

The Merchant of Yonkers, 1938.

The Skin of Our Teeth, 1942.
The Shadow of a Doubt (screenplay for Alfred Hitchcock film), 1942.

The Ides of March, 1948.

The Matchmaker (revised text of The Merchant of Yonkers), 1954.

Plays for Bleeker Street (Someone from Assisi; Infancy; Childhood), 1962.

Hello, Dolly! (musical comedy adaptation of The Matchmaker), 1964.

The Eighth Day, 1967.

Theophilus North, 1973.

The Alcestiad. Published posthumously, 1977.

American Characteristics and Other Essays. Collected and published posthumously, 1979.

WORKS ABOUT

Thornton Wilder

Blank, Martin, ed. *Critical Essays on Thornton Wilder*. New York: G. K. Hall & Co., 1996.

Broussard, Louis. *American Drama: Contemporary Allegory from Eugene O'Neill to Tennessee Williams*. Norman, Oklahoma: University of Oklahoma Press, 1962.

Burbank, Rex. *Thornton Wilder*, 2nd edition. Boston: Twayne Publishers, 1961.

Campbell, Joseph, and Henry M. Robinson. "The Skin of Whose Teeth?" *Saturday Review of Literature* XXV (19 December 1942): pp. 3-4.

Castronovo, David. *Thornton Wilder*. New York: Ungar Publishing Company, 1986.

Corrigan, Robert W. *The Theatre in Search of a Fix*. New York: Dell Publishing Co. Inc., 1973.

Desmastes, William W. ed. *Realism and the American Tradition*. Tuscaloosa and London: University of Alabama Press, 1996.

Fuller, Edmund. "Reappraisals: Thornton Wilder: 'The Notation of the Heart'" *The American Scholar* XXVIII (Spring 1959): pp. 210-217.

Fulton, A. R. "Expressionism—Twenty Years After." *Sewanee Review* LII (Summer 1944): pp. 398-413.

Gassner, John. *Form and Idea in Modern Theatre*. New York: The Dryden Press, 1956.

Gold, Michael. "Prophet of the Genteel Christ." *The New Republic* LXIV (22 October 1930): pp.266-267.

Goldstein, Malcolm. *The Art of Thornton Wilder*. Lincoln: University of Nebraska Press, 1965.

Grebanier, *Thornton Wilder*. Minneapolis: University of Minnesota Press, 1964.

Guthrie, Tyrone. *A life in the Theatre*. New York: McGraw-Hill Publishing Co.,1959.

Haberman, Donald. *Our Town: American Play*. Boston: Twayne Publishers, 1989.

―――. *The Plays of Thornton Wilder: a Critical Study*. Middletown, CT: Wesleyan University Press, 1967.

Harrison. Gilbert A. *The Enthusiast: A life of Thornton Wilder*. New Haven and New York: Ticknor & Fields, 1983.

Kernan, Alvin B. *The Modern American Theatre: A Collection of Critical Essays*. Englewood Cliffs, NJ: Prentice-Hall, Inc., 1967.

Kuner, M.C. *Thornton Wilder: The Bright and the Dark*. New York: Thomas Y. Crowell Company, 1972.

MacCleish, Archibald. "The Isolation of the American Artist." *Atlantic Monthly* (January 1958): pp.55-59.

McCarthy, Mary. *Sights and Spectacles: 1937-1936*. New York: Farrar, Straus and Cudhahy, 1956.

―――. "Theatre Chronicle." *Partisan Review* IV (April 1938): pp.55-56.

Miller, Arthur. "The Family in Modern Drama." *Atlantic Monthly* (April 1956): pp. 34-44.

Popper, Hermine O. "The Universe of Thornton Wilder." *Harper's Magazine* 230 (June 1965): pp.72-81.

Scott, Winfield Townley. *Exiles and Fabrications*. Garden City, New York: Doubleday & Company, Inc., 1961.

Simon, Linda. *Thornton Wilder: His World*. Garden City, New York: Doubleday & Company Inc., 1979.

Wescott, Glenway. *Images of Truth: Remembrances and New Criticism*. New York and Evanston: Harper & Row Publishers, 1962.

Wilson, Edmund. *The Shores of Light*. New York: Farrar, Straus and Young, Inc., 1952.

ACKNOWLEDGMENTS

The Shores of Light by Edmund Wilson © 1952 by Farrar, Straus and Young, Inc. Reprinted by Permission of Farrar, Straus and Giroux.

"The World of Thornton Wilder" by Tyrone Guthrie from *The Modern American Theatre*, ed. Alvin B. Kernan. © 1967 by Prentice-Hall, Inc. Reprinted with Permission.

"The Man Who Abolished Time" by Malcolm Cowley from *Critical Essays on Thornton Wilder*, ed. Martin Blank © 1956 by G. K. Hall. Reprinted by permission of The Gale Group.

"Joyce and the Modern Novel" by Thornton Wilder. From *American Characteristics and Other Essays* © 1979, 2000 by Estate of Thornton Wilder. Reprinted by arrangment with The Wilder Family LLC and The Barbara Hogenson Agency, Inc. All rights reserved.

From *Thornton Wilder* by Rex Burbank. © 1978 by G.K. Hall. Reprinted by permission of The Gale Group.

"The Notations of the Heart" by Edmund Fuller from *Critical Essays on Thornton Wilder*, ed. Martin Blank. © 1956 by G.K. Hall. Reprinted by permission of The Gale Group.

Mrs. Lyndon B. Johnson, included in "The World of Thornton Wilder." *Harper's Magazine* 230 (June, 1965). Reprinted with Permission.

"The Universe of Thornton Wilder" by Hermine I. Popper from *Harper's Magazine* 230, (June, 1965). Reprinted with Permission.

The Theatre in Search of a Fix by Robert W. Corrigano. © 1973 by Robert W. Corrigano. Used by permission of Dell Publishing, a division of Random House, Inc.

"Expressionism—Twenty Years After" by A.R. Fulton. First published in the *Sewanee Review*, vol 52, no 3, summer 1944. Reprinted with Permission.

"The Family in Modern Drama" by Arthur Miller from *Atlantic Monthly* 197 (April, 1956). Reprinted by permission of International Creative Management, Inc. © 1956 by Arthur Miller. First appeared in *Atlantic Monthly*.

Exiles and Fabrications by Winfield Townley Scott. © 1961 by Doubleday & Company, Inc. Reprinted with Permission.

Themes of Ideas